THE BIBLE IN 52 WEEKS FOR TEEN GIRLS

the BIBLE
IN 52 WEEKS
FOR TEEN GIRLS

A YEARLONG BIBLE STUDY

BRITTANY RUST

callisto publishing
an imprint of Sourcebooks

Copyright © 2025 by Callisto Publishing LLC
Cover and internal design © 2025 by Callisto Publishing LLC
Illustrations by Agnieszka Żylińska-Rękas; © Bibela/Creative Market
Author photo courtesy of Christian Gideon
Series Designer: Liz Cosgrove
Art Director: Lisa Schreiber
Art Producer: Stacey Stambaugh
Editor: Rachel Poloski
Production Editor: Rachel Taenzler
Production Designer: Martin Worthington

Callisto Teens and the colophon are registered trademarks of Callisto Publishing LLC.

All rights reserved. No part of this book may be reproduced in any form or by any electronic or mechanical means including information storage and retrieval systems—except in the case of brief quotations embodied in critical articles or reviews—without permission in writing from its publisher, Sourcebooks LLC.

All biblical verses are used as reflected in the New International Version (NIV) of the Christian Bible unless otherwise noted.

Published by Callisto Publishing LLC C/O Sourcebooks LLC

P.O. Box 4410, Naperville, Illinois 60567-4410
(630) 961-3900
callistopublishing.com

Library of Congress Cataloging-in-Publication Data

Names: Rust, Brittany, author.
Title: The Bible in 52 weeks for teen girls : a yearlong Bible study / Brittany Rust.
Other titles: Bible in fifty two weeks for teen girls
Description: Naperville, Illinois : Callisto Publishing, [2025] | Series: Bible in 52 weeks | Includes index.
Identifiers: LCCN 2024048844 (trade paperback) | LCCN 2024048845 (epub)
Subjects: LCSH: Bible--Devotional literature. | Bible--Study and teaching. | Teenage girls--Religious life.
Classification: LCC BS491.5 .R87 2025 (print) | LCC BS491.5 (ebook) | DDC 242/.633--dc23/eng/20250107
LC record available at https://lccn.loc.gov/2024048844
LC ebook record available at https://lccn.loc.gov/2024048845

Printed and bound in China.
OGP 10 9 8 7 6 5 4 3 2 1

To the One who saw a lost sixteen-year-old girl and rescued her.

CONTENTS

Introduction ix
How to Use This Book xi

WEEK 1: **GOING BACK TO WHERE IT STARTED** 2

WEEK 2: **WHEN TRUST IS TESTED** 6

WEEK 3: **OVERLOOKED BUT NOT FORGOTTEN** 10

WEEK 4: **DON'T DOUBT WHAT GOD CAN DO** 14

WEEK 5: **A GOOD THING OR A GOD THING?** 18

WEEK 6: **STANDING OUT IN THE WORLD** 22

WEEK 7: **CARVING YOUR PATH** 26

WEEK 8: **GOD IS A REFUGE** 30

WEEK 9: **DO NOT FEAR** 33

WEEK 10: **DEFINED BY GOD, NOT YOUR PAST** 37

WEEK 11: **PEACE OVER FEAR** 41

WEEK 12: **SHELTER UNDER HIS WINGS** 44

WEEK 13: **FAITHFULNESS OVER FADS** 48

WEEK 14: **QUICK TO REPENT** 51

WEEK 15: **HANDLING THE UPS AND DOWNS** 54

WEEK 16: **YOUR FIRST FOCUS** 58

WEEK 17: **FIND YOUR PEOPLE** 61

WEEK 18: **STANDING IN GOD WHEN YOU'RE WORRIED** 65

WEEK 19: **FAVOR TO THE HUMBLE** 68

WEEK 20: **YOU WERE MADE FOR NOW** 71

WEEK 21: **WISDOM FOR YOUR SUFFERING** 74

WEEK 22: **PEACE IN A PERSON** 78

WEEK 23: **DIRECTING YOUR THOUGHTS** 81

WEEK 24: **LEADING YOUR EMOTIONS** 85

WEEK 25: **WHY THINGS CAN GET HARD** 88

WEEK 26: **WEATHERING THE STORM** 91

WEEK 27: **GOING TO GOD OUT OF DESIRE** 94

WEEK 28: **LIVING WISELY** 97

WEEK 29: **THE PROVERBS 31 WOMAN** 101

WEEK 30: **LOVE IN THE BIBLE** 105

WEEK 31: **USING YOUR GIFTS GOD'S WAY** 109

WEEK 32: **ANOINTED TO DO GOOD WORKS** 112

WEEK 33: **BEING A WITNESS** 116

WEEK 34: **THE ONLY CURE FOR YOUR PAIN** 119

WEEK 35: **A TOTAL CHANGE OF HEART** 122

WEEK 36: **COURAGE AGAINST THE CULTURE** 126

WEEK 37: **A DOOR OF HOPE** 130

WEEK 38: **THE COST OF DISOBEDIENCE** 134

WEEK 39: **CONSIDER YOUR WAYS** 137

WEEK 40: **THE REASON THIS BOOK CHANGES YOU** 140

WEEK 41: **THE GREAT COMMANDMENT** 143

WEEK 42: **THE WORLD DOESN'T HAVE IT** 147

WEEK 43: **REJECTED FOR YOUR FAITH** 151

WEEK 44: **LEARNING FROM OTHERS** 154

WEEK 45: **HOW TO LIVE AS A CHRISTIAN** 157

WEEK 46: **WARNING AGAINST SIN AND TEMPTATION** 160

WEEK 47: **THE COMPARISON TRAP** 163

WEEK 48: **BATTLING YOUR THOUGHTS** 166

WEEK 49: **OVERCOMING FEAR** 169

WEEK 50: **HEARING AND DOING** 172

WEEK 51: **EFFECTIVE PRAYER** 176

WEEK 52: **LIVING WITH ETERNITY IN MIND** 179

Group Study Guide 185

Resources 187

Index 188

INTRODUCTION

HI THERE! MY NAME IS BRITTANY, and this book is for you. You're likely reading this because you desire something more. Or should I say, Someone more. Maybe you don't know what, who, or where that is in this moment, but I pray that by the end of this book, you will.

    I didn't grow up in a Christian home, but I always believed there was something more to life that I was missing. When I was sixteen years old, that all changed when a friend invited me to a local youth group, and I heard the Gospel preached for the first time. Instantly, I knew my life was forever changed, and it really has been since that day. God has been so good and faithful to me, even when I haven't been good or faithful to Him.

    When that change happened, I consumed the Bible and anything I could get my hands on to help grow my faith. The reason? I knew nothing about God or the Bible, so learning as much as I could seemed the best place to start. Honestly, there wasn't much out there that was appealing for a teenage girl. But here I am, years later, ready to take all that I've learned and hand it to you for your benefit. This book truly is for you, so you can have what I didn't, and I pray it will be such a blessing!

    Reading and journaling were some of the best things I did back then, and I continue to do both now. God has all this wisdom for how to live, and all this guidance to protect His daughters in a world that often hurts. Reading about it in the Bible daily has changed my life, and I know it will for you as well.

By reading God's Word, combing through these pages, and writing down your thoughts, you are investing in a holy life, one that radiates the love of God and serves others in the process. It's a journey that will help you navigate all the challenges you face.

I pray that this book, which will tackle so many of the things you face daily, will equip you for the kind of life that God blesses, and that you will grow in your understanding of God and His Word in huge ways. One year from now you'll be able to trace—because you stayed in your readings and wrote it all down along the way—how God moved in your life. I truly believe He will. In fact, the Bible says His Word, when it goes out, will accomplish His purpose.

So is my word that goes out from my mouth: It will not return to me empty, but will accomplish what I desire and achieve the purpose for which I sent it. ▶ Isaiah 55:11

HOW TO USE THIS BOOK

THIS BOOK IS MEANT TO BE YOUR partner for the next year and, as a companion to the Bible, it will be a beautiful resource you can introduce into your devotional time. It will teach you more than you can imagine and shepherd you into a deeper relationship with God, all leading to a more fulfilling life. Which brings me to a very important note: Your Bible is your primary source of reading to know God and His Word. Use it first. Use it most. Then reach for this book to nourish your soul and add to what God is speaking to your heart and mind.

This book will provide a study of Scripture, along with practical applications you can use in your daily life. It's in my heart to be God's conduit in equipping you with words that will help you navigate faith, relationships, identity, and your calling.

You will work through the Bible and hit every book: Old Testament and New Testament. So, to map it out for you: There are sixty-six books in the Bible. Of those, thirty-nine are Old Testament books and twenty-seven are from the New Testament. Now, you might be wondering: What's the difference? Basically, the Old Testament covers God's history from Creation up until the birth of Jesus, and the New Testament covers the time of Jesus through the early church.

You'll see the verses in NIV (New International Version) form, but use whatever translation you have at home. There are also ways to read or listen to the Bible on your phone or computer—there are so many options.

Have your Bible near you as you read this book, to highlight interesting verses and to take notes in it about what you're learning. I love marking up my Bible and writing notes about the verses I'm reading. By doing so, I can always quickly refer back to what God taught me. So, as you prepare to start this awesome journey, grab your favorite highlighters and pens, a journal, and your Bible. Seriously, having your own Bible "kit" ready to go will be a great way to study. Write down what you're learning and how you're growing, and it will be a treasure you come back to for years to come.

As I mentioned, you will be covering the whole Bible, and by reading in the order I have laid out, you will get a strong grasp of the themes and the story of God's Word. I've covered several topics that are at the core of a teenage girl's life, such as identity, faith, relationships, and more. Believe me, I remember those years, and I'm sharing with you many things I wish I had known back then.

The daily readings are for fifty-two weeks, six days a week, but don't worry if you can't do it every day—I get it, life happens. Each devotional should take about fifteen minutes to read, but take more time if you need to. And remember, the enemy doesn't want you on this path. There will be days that blow by, when it will be hard to find time or when disruptions will get in your way. If on some (or all) days you find it challenging to open the Bible, listen to an audio version of it. The point is: There is a way! Don't give up. Stay committed. Keep going and watch God do something really neat in your life. I promise you the commitment will be totally worth it.

Before I leave you to begin your journey, I want to encourage you: This will be a beautiful year if you stay in the process. I believe God will meet with you and speak to you in ways you have not encountered yet. It's true: The more you know God, the more you love God. So, dive deep, friend. Commit to the journey and know that I lift you in prayer with the hope of you coming out on the other side of this a different person. God is good, and He is faithful.

WHAT MATERIALS DO I NEED?

This book.

The Bible. Use any version you want. The verses in this book are from the New International Version (NIV), but I also really like the ESV (English Standard Version). You may also like an audio version on your phone.

Notebook, journal, or tablet. This will be helpful if you want to take extra notes. I encourage this since I have always benefited from writing down what I'm learning.

A pen or pencil and highlighters. Feel free to mark up this book and your Bible along the way.

WHAT'S IN THIS BOOK?

This book is your guide to discovering the beauty and truths of the Bible. You will work your way through the entire Bible in fifty-two weeks, or one year. Each week, there will be six daily Bible readings with lightly guided reflection questions. The seventh day can be used to catch up or for further reflection.

I've purposely built in the seventh "buffer" day in case you miss one or get behind. There's no need to get frustrated or give up. Use your "days off" to jump back in and keep going. I can tell you that as with any habit, the more you do, the easier it will get.

Not only do I provide daily Bible readings for you, but I also include rich commentary to help you understand what is happening in the Scripture, reflective prompts, and a rotating bonus section that you can apply to your everyday life.

You won't be reading the Bible in chronological order (although that's my favorite way), but rather by how it's laid out. This way, you can see the themes and big picture. By the time you're done, you will have read the whole Bible.

GREAT IN A GROUP OR ON YOUR OWN

You may use this book primarily as a personal devotion or study, and that's great. It's perfect for your time with God each day. But you can also get a group of friends together, or meet with a mentor or parent, and use it in a group setting. There is a Group Study Guide at the end of the book with questions and weekly prompts to help promote meaningful group conversation.

YOU CAN DO IT!

Finding time each day to be with God can be a challenge. We live in a world full of distractions. But I know a powerful truth, because I've seen it play out in my own life: The more time you spend in His Word, the more He will shape a God-flourishing life.

So, I encourage you—make time. Maybe that means getting up twenty minutes earlier. That's how I do it, because I know if I don't  spend that time in the morning, chances are good I won't do it at all. But maybe you're a night owl and prefer the quiet moments of the evening. Try that. Find what works best for you. I hope this book conveys that I'm here for *you*. I hope it encourages you, and I hope it helps you soak up Scripture in your devotions.

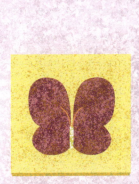

WEEK 1
GOING BACK TO WHERE IT STARTED

DAILY READINGS

- Day 1: Genesis 1–3
- Day 2: Genesis 4–6
- Day 3: Genesis 7–9
- Day 4: Genesis 10–11
- Day 5: Genesis 12–14
- **Day 6: Genesis 15–16**
- Day 7: Catch up on any readings you've missed.

WE'RE STARTING AT THE BEGINNING—God's creation in Genesis. There's no better place for you to begin this journey than when time itself kicked off! Did you know that's what "Genesis" means: "in the beginning"? Which is exactly how verse 1 launches. In the first eleven chapters, we read about God's work during Creation, the Fall, the Flood, and the scattering of people. Then we hit chapter 12, and from there, the rest of the book looks at the family God chose to bring His people from: Abraham, Isaac, and Jacob.

That's the background of what we're looking at this week. It's a book rich in history and stories. In fact, it's one of my favorite books in the Bible for those two reasons. And honestly, I wish I could cover each chapter in depth with you, because it's that good.

But if there's one thing that stands out most in these chapters, it's God's desire to be in a relationship with people. Yes, it's true. God created us for that purpose, and He's continued to make a way for us to have that beautiful connection, even when we don't deserve it. He didn't need us around; He *wanted* us around. Even after sin entered the picture (see chapter 3), God created a way to right people's sins through atonement, to make right any wrongs that were done. He didn't have to, but again, He *wanted* to because He desired (and still desires) a relationship with all people, including you and me.

Even in the Flood, God didn't wipe us out completely. That's mercy. In the rebellion at the Tower of Babel, He scattered the people rather than get rid of them. That's mercy, too. He did this because of His profound love for people. And we see that most clearly with Abram, or Abraham, starting in chapter 12. You're going to witness a really sweet connection between God and Abram. Did Abram make mistakes? Definitely. But his faith was in God. Genesis 15:6 says he *believed the Lord, and he credited it to him as righteousness.*

Abram trusted God, and that was the basis for their relationship.

As you read this week, look for evidence of God's mercy, grace, and desire for a relationship with His people. It's a beautiful theme and one I really hope inspires you to trust God. Because when you do, no matter what comes, you'll be held firm in your faith, and God will carry you through.

REWIND AND REJOICE

1. Looking at the first eleven chapters, from Creation until Abram, what do you notice about God's desire for people? What stands out the most?

   _____

   _____

   _____

2. Would you say you fully trust God? If so, how has that become important in your life? If not, write down why and/or in what areas of your life you see that lack of trust.

   _____

   _____

   _____

3. What are you hoping to see happen in your walk with God over the next year?

   _____

   _____

   _____

AND I PRAY

Dear Lord,
Thank You for the Bible and the guidance You've given me. I'm excited to take this journey and get to know You and Your Word better. Help me soak up all Your teaching and grow in my faith. And help me, please, learn how to trust You more. I want to be so sure of You and our relationship. Amen.

WEEK 2
WHEN TRUST IS TESTED

DAILY READINGS

- Day 1: Genesis 17–19
- **Day 2: Genesis 20–22**
- Day 3: Genesis 23–25
- Day 4: Genesis 26–28
- Day 5: Genesis 29–31
- Day 6: Genesis 32–34
- Day 7: Catch up on any readings you've missed.

THE FIRST TIME my trust in God was *really* tested was not long after I graduated high school. I felt a strong calling to do a discipleship program. But the program cost money and I didn't have much. I saved as much as I could, but within a week of the program starting, I didn't have enough. I thought I would have to drop out, and I was devastated. But God provided through the parents of a friend. That went on to happen three times during the nine months I was in the program.

Have you ever been sure about something, but then it didn't work out how you needed it to? Or how you initially hoped it would? And then at the last minute, God stepped in and answered. Or maybe you're even in that moment now, and your faith is being stretched.

Abraham knew what it was like to have his faith tested. In chapter 22, we see he finally has his biggest dream come true: He has a son. It took a long time, decades of waiting, to get there. And then he had the son he always prayed for. But in chapter 22, God does something surprising: He tells Abraham to sacrifice his son.

Now, it might seem wild that God asked Abraham to sacrifice his son, but God was testing Abraham. He wanted to make sure Abraham hadn't made his son an idol. That he hadn't put his son before God.

What did Abraham do? He immediately took his son to a mountain, put him on an altar, and almost sacrificed him—and then God stepped in. You might be wondering: How could Abraham have done that? Well, it went back to the promise God made to him in chapters 15 and 17. God promised He would give the man a son, and Abraham believed God.

So here, Abraham remembered what God promised him about his son, Isaac. Hebrews 11:19 tells us that he was so sure about God that even if God had to raise Isaac from the dead, he would. You might say that's a massive theme in the life of Abraham—having the faith to trust God when things seem uncertain. In situations where Abraham was stretched, he ultimately learned to trust God. And you know what? God will do the same in your life to make sure your faith and trust in Him are strong.

Think about things in your life that are hard and are stretching beyond what you can handle. Will you learn to trust God to take care of you, no matter what?

REWIND AND REJOICE

1. Are you shocked by God's command in Genesis 22? Does looking back at the prophecies in chapters 15 and 17 help you better understand what happened?

   _____

   _____

   _____

2. Is there something in your life you put before God or think of more than you think of God?

   _____

   _____

   _____

3. How might you get rid of an idol in your life?

   _____

   _____

   _____

BIBLE TRUTHS

Isaac wasn't Abraham's first son—that was actually Ishmael. But Ishmael was born because Abraham and Sarah took matters into their own hands instead of trusting God. Even so, God took care of Ishmael and his mother, Hagar. This shows us that God cares about all people and extends mercy without prejudice. If you're wondering if He loves you, I can confidently say He does.

WEEK 3
OVERLOOKED BUT NOT FORGOTTEN

DAILY READINGS

- Day 1: Genesis 35–37
- **Day 2: Genesis 38–40**
- Day 3: Genesis 41–43
- Day 4: Genesis 44–46
- Day 5: Genesis 47–48
- Day 6: Genesis 49–50
- Day 7: Catch up on any readings you've missed.

HAVE YOU EVER FELT OVERLOOKED or forgotten? It's easy to feel this way, whether it's in a lunchroom or during a basketball game. Or maybe you've felt unnoticed in a big family with lots going on at the dinner table. When you feel lost in the crowd, you might struggle to see what your purpose is or how you can make a difference.

A guy in the Bible, Joseph, who was a great-grandson of Abraham, may have felt something similar. He was the second youngest of twelve boys, and his brothers didn't like him much. He definitely had outsider vibes.

One day, he went to his brothers out in the country, and they sold him into slavery. Joseph was carried hundreds of miles from his home to Egypt. While a slave, he earned the trust of his master and was put in charge of the household. Yet when he did the right thing, he was punished and sent to prison. He thrived in prison, too, and ended up in charge of the other prisoners.

So, let's stop here. You have a guy from a wealthy family, but his brothers betrayed him and sent him to be a slave. He did well and did the right thing but was sent to prison anyway. It seems like it went from bad to worse for Joseph, right?

Joseph is actually my favorite person in the Bible, outside of Jesus (obviously!), because he was so determined in his faith and loved God intensely, even in adversity. Put yourself in his shoes. You may have thought that life was getting worse and worse, and you may have questioned God. But the truth is, each setback brought Joseph closer to his calling.

See, back home, God gave Joseph dreams that he would one day lead. But realistically, how could he do that without leadership experience? As a slave, he led a large household. In prison, he ran an extensive system. God prepared him for something bigger and opened an amazing door for him to become second in command over the largest country in that part of the world. That never would have happened if Joseph had stayed home.

Sometimes it may feel like God doesn't see you. Or things just get worse for you, even when you do the right thing. If Joseph's life shows us anything, it's that God does see and is faithful. Be like Joseph: Seek God and do the right thing. Eventually, you'll see God bring together all the puzzle pieces and reveal what His big plan for you looks like. The hidden places can become the best places for growing into who God made you to be.

REWIND AND REJOICE

1. Does any part of Joseph's story feel relatable to something you've been through? What and how?

   _____
   _____
   _____

2. Does something in your life right now feel like a struggle even though you are doing the right thing?

   _____
   _____
   _____

3. How can Joseph's story encourage you to keep going?

   _____
   _____
   _____

LIVE IN LIGHT

1. Trust God to take whatever you are going through and use it for His good plan.

2. Notice how situations or moments in your life are working together toward a bigger picture. This is a great journal activity to keep up so you can reflect on your journey with God.

3. Someone else around you might be struggling to feel seen. Encourage one person this week by showing them kindness.

WEEK 4
DON'T DOUBT WHAT GOD CAN DO

DAILY READINGS

- **Day 1: Exodus 1–4**
- **Day 2: Exodus 5–9**
- Day 3: Exodus 10–13
- Day 4: Exodus 14–17
- Day 5: Exodus 18–21
- Day 6: Exodus 22–24
- Day 7: Catch up on any readings you've missed.

EXODUS IS A BOOK FULL of the miraculous. It's an account of God's people, who were in slavery in Egypt for four hundred years before leaving and making their way to the land God promised them. We see God send plagues, part the sea, send bread from the sky, and so much more.

But we also see a lot of people doubt God's good plans. So, you know how there's a part of you that wonders if He is working in your life or if He can be trusted? That part of you will *definitely* want to read what happens next.

To set His people free, God chose Moses. Now, Moses was a Hebrew, but by God's design, he ended up in Pharoah's house. He had everything anyone in the world could want. But he risked it all in one moment by killing an Egyptian who was cruel to a Hebrew slave. So, Moses ran away into the wilderness and spent forty years taking care of sheep.

While Moses was in the middle of nowhere, God spoke to him from a burning bush. He called Moses to return to Egypt and lead God's people out of Egypt and to the Promised Land. But Moses had some doubts—five to be exact—as noted in Exodus 4–5.

Listen, doubts will pop up. Should I go to this school, or help that friend, or take a step of faith? It isn't a sin to have questions, as long as you bring them to God and deal with them the right way. And the cool thing is, He can handle them. This passage gives you great direction for dealing with those exact moments.

You know what God told Moses to consider when he was doubting? Well, He had a lot to say, but here are five things He wanted Moses to think about:

1. God is the only qualification you need.
2. Maybe He is doing something new or different you aren't familiar with.
3. He will provide what you need.
4. He will equip you.
5. He will send people to walk the journey with you.

Maybe God is asking you to let go of a hobby or sport so you can focus on Him. It may not make sense, but you can bet that if you're committing to God over the material world, it will be worth it. Or perhaps it's the opposite: You're trying out for a school sport but doubting your ability. Whatever happens, God has a great plan for your life.

I hope this week's readings help you believe in God's plan for you, and I pray you don't doubt what that is or if He is with you. With God on your side, you can overcome doubt by trusting His faithfulness.

REWIND AND REJOICE

1. Moses had five doubts—which do you think you might lean toward?

_____
_____
_____
_____

2. Describe when you felt doubt held (or tried to hold) you back. How could you have handled it differently?

_____

_____

_____

_____

3. How would you handle doubt today?

_____

_____

_____

_____

VERSE FOCUS

I am the Lord, and I will bring you out from under the yoke of the Egyptians. I will free you from being slaves to them, and I will redeem you with an outstretched arm and with mighty acts of judgment. I will take you as my own people, and I will be your God. Then you will know that I am the Lord your God, who brought you out from under the yoke of the Egyptians. ▶ **Exodus 6:6–7**

WEEK 5
A GOOD THING OR A GOD THING?

DAILY READINGS

- Day 1: Exodus 25–28
- **Day 2: Exodus 29–32**
- Day 3: Exodus 33–36
- Day 4: Exodus 37–40
- Day 5: Leviticus 1–4
- Day 6: Leviticus 5–7
- Day 7: Catch up on any readings you've missed.

GOOD NEWS: THE PEOPLE are finally out of Egypt! The bad news: They have to spend forty years in the wilderness before entering the Promised Land. And a ton happens along the way.

    One thing you're going to see is that the people fumble a lot. They were called to devote themselves to God, but they grumbled when they didn't have the food they wanted, complained when life wasn't easy, and made idols out of flashy things (sounds a lot like today, huh?). And that's what I'd like to talk about now: the golden calf in Exodus 32. Moses went to the top of the mountain to get God's Law, and while he was gone, the people took their gold, made an idol, and worshipped it. This story highlights the theme that the Israelites were sort of half in with God but still half in with the world. And it's easier, and more subtle, to worship an idol than you think.

    So, what is an idol? It isn't always a statue. In fact, it rarely is. Idols are things in your life you put before your relationship with God. Something or someone you think of and care more about than you think of or care about God. Which is why it can be more subtle than you think. It's not always a physical monument; it could be a monument of the heart. It could be a boyfriend (usually a major idol for teenage girl), a sport you play, perfect grades, or looking a certain way to fit into the "in" crowd. These are all ways you can put someone or something before God.

    Want to know what mine is? Ministry. Yep! I'm more careful now than I used to be, but there was a time when I would make ministry my idol. You might be thinking, that doesn't seem like an idol; it's a good thing. Yes, ministry is a good thing, but even good things can become

A GOOD THING OR A GOD THING?

god things if we aren't careful. Once you and I make something a god thing—meaning, we put them before God—it becomes an idol. And idols are dangerous. God despises idols because He has called us to worship Him only.

What in your life might be or become an idol? Think about the good things that drive you or take up all your thoughts. And then size them up against how much you pursue God. That will give you a pretty good idea of where your heart is. And if something seems to be overshadowing God, do you have the commitment to God to root it out of your heart?

God wants your whole heart. Are you willing to give it to Him?

REWIND AND REJOICE

1. What are your initial thoughts when reading this account in Exodus 32?

   _____
   _____
   _____

2. Spend some time reflecting on potential idols in your life. Are there any, and how will you respond to them?

   _____
   _____
   _____

3. Is there something you can do to guard your heart from idols?

_____
_____
_____

AND I PRAY

Dear Lord,
I love You and want to give You my whole heart. Sometimes, that's hard because there are people and situations that want to get in the way, but I reject those things. I want to follow You alone. Please help me to make You first in my life. Amen.

WEEK 6
STANDING OUT IN THE WORLD

DAILY READINGS

- Day 1: Leviticus 8–10
- Day 2: Leviticus 11–14
- Day 3: Leviticus 15–17
- **Day 4: Leviticus 18–20**
- Day 5: Leviticus 21–24
- Day 6: Leviticus 25–27
- Day 7: Catch up on any readings you've missed.

LEVITICUS CAN BE A TOUGH one, so you're not alone if reading it feels a bit harder to you. But can I encourage you? Every part and every word in the Bible has value and purpose for your life. Sometimes, it just takes a little more digging to see what that is, and Leviticus is that kind of book.

To help give some insight into what's happening here, it's mainly a book of religious practices and commands for the priests, which might feel outdated for how we live today. And with the New Testament making most of the practices in Leviticus no longer necessary because of grace, many might wonder what value it holds today.

Yes, Leviticus is ancient, but that doesn't mean it has no value in your life. The theme of God's righteousness is present, and if you pay attention, you can learn about His character in these pages.

Written by Moses, Leviticus addresses the responsibilities of the Levites and priests, and notes practices that helped people connect with God and live a holy life.

You must remember that Israel had just come out of the land of Egypt. For hundreds of years, the culture they lived in worshipped many gods, and a sort of watered-down version of true religion had become their norm. They were confused. God gave them in Leviticus a clear picture of His will and desire for how they should live.

But what I want you to focus on—instead of the law—is God's holy character. See in it your tendency to sin and need for atonement. The atonement for your sin has changed (Jesus instead of ritual), but the need for it has not.

Focus on Leviticus 20:26 *You are to be holy to me because I, the Lord, am holy, and I have set you apart from the nations to be my own.* God is holy, and you are called to be holy, too. And what that basically means is set apart. You are to look and act differently from the world, the people at your school, and what you see on TV. God is totally different, isn't He? Well, so you are to be as well. So, if this book feels heavy at times, slow down and ask yourself, "What does this teach me about God and a holy life?" Don't worry about getting all the commands figured out; focus on His character and the kind of character He wants in a person.

REWIND AND REJOICE

1. What is your definition of holy, or how do you think about it right now?

   _____
   _____
   _____

2. How does God look different from the world?

   _____
   _____
   _____

3. Is there something in your life that looks too much like the world? How could you change it to look more like God?

   _____
   _____
   _____

BIBLE TRUTHS

You heard me say that much of what we see in Leviticus isn't needed anymore. Do you know why? Because of Jesus. When He died on the cross for our sins, He became the perfect sacrifice once and for all. So, instead of making offerings on an altar or celebrating feasts, we worship Jesus.

WEEK 7
CARVING YOUR PATH

DAILY READINGS

- [ ] Day 1: Numbers 1–3
- [ ] Day 2: Numbers 4–6
- [ ] Day 3: Numbers 7–10
- [ ] **Day 4: Numbers 11–13**
- [ ] Day 5: Numbers 14–16
- [ ] Day 6: Numbers 17–20
- [ ] Day 7: Catch up on any readings you've missed.

ISRAEL REALLY DROPS the ball in Numbers 13. The people wanted confirmation that the Promised Land was good, so they encouraged Moses to send spies to the area. Those spies discovered the amazing fruits of the land, but they also observed intimidating men carrying those fruits. So, most of the spies came back to Moses and essentially said, "We can't do this."

Joshua and Caleb believed they could go up against those men with God, but it wasn't enough to sway the rebellious people of Israel. So what did God do? He announced that He would disinherit the people. Moses interceded on their behalf, and God relented.

But there were consequences to their disobedience: They had to wander the wilderness for forty years. Yet, even in that, God took care of them by providing shade, food, water, and more. And in Numbers we see an older generation of disobedient people die off and a new generation grow up following God.

There's so much here we can look at. That God took the disobedient, unbelieving people of Numbers 14 and made a new start with them. That unbelief led to bad consequences. But also there is this bigger truth that we don't have to repeat the sins of the people who have gone before us.

We all have or have had people impact how we think, feel, and act. Many people in my family get angry easily, and I fight every day to overcome my own anger. I have friends who stay away from alcohol because an uncle or parent drinks too much. I don't know if there is a struggle in your family you may have to fight against, but if there is, I encourage you to do so today through His word.

You are not the person who has gone before you, good or bad. You get to make your own choices. And with one prayer the Holy Spirit can flood in and help you with problems you can't solve on your own. Take what you're learning in the Bible, ask God to help you apply it, and grow into the girl God is making you to be.

REWIND AND REJOICE

1. Have you ever felt a bit like the Israelites after the spies came back? Worried, afraid, or avoidant? Did you complain about it?

   _____
   _____
   _____

2. Does anything in your life feel like a dark shadow following you—maybe family struggles or a mistake you made? Do you really want to break free? What is it and where does it come from?

   _____
   _____
   _____

3. What can you do to overcome that dark cloud and live in the light?

   _____
   _____
   _____

LIVE IN LIGHT

1. Focus on not complaining when you're afraid or something doesn't go your way. Instead, choose to be thankful for the good. Feeling gratitude is a great way to overcome fear.

2. Take your response from the third Rewind and Rejoice question and try to practice it this week.

WEEK 8
GOD IS A REFUGE

DAILY READINGS

- Day 1: Numbers 21–24
- Day 2: Numbers 25–28
- Day 3: Numbers 29–32
- **Day 4: Numbers 33–36**
- Day 5: Deuteronomy 1–4
- Day 6: Deuteronomy 5–8
- Day 7: Catch up on any readings you've missed.

GOD IS YOUR REFUGE, your safe place. When you're afraid, hurting, confused, or lost, the best place to run is to God. Which is exactly what we're going to see in the text this week.

One of the cool things about the Old Testament is that it's all real stories about real events. And if you like history, it's fascinating. But there are also things in the Bible that serve as images of something else, allegories or second meanings. We see that in Numbers 35, and they're called refuge cities.

For the new land they were about to take, God wanted to make sure the people set aside six refuge cities for asylum seekers. So basically, if you killed someone but it was an accident, you could seek safety there until judgment could be passed down.

These refuge cities served as images of God. The Bible applies this parallel between the refuge city and the believer finding refuge in God on more than one occasion. We run to Jesus to find safety from the dangers we face because of sin, God's wrath, and the reality of hell. Only Jesus can give us refuge from these things, and we must turn to Him alone. Just as the cities of refuge were open to anyone seeking safety, Jesus protects everyone who comes to Him to escape sin and its punishment.

I don't know where you stand with Jesus today. But I do know He is a refuge from this world, a safe place in the storm. And He wants to take all your sins upon Himself and redeem you from an eternity without God. The work has already been done on the cross. It's now your decision to choose between following Him or following this world.

If you have decided to follow Christ, that's absolutely wonderful. If you haven't, it's not too late. At this moment He is calling your name and inviting you to love, know, and follow Him. But He won't make that decision for you. Neither can anyone else.

Do you want to make Him the Lord of your life? I hope so! And if you do, confess your sin, ask for His forgiveness, and tell Him you want to follow Him. That's it! Find a good church and community, and I'll be here to walk out the rest of the year with you in this faith.

REWIND AND REJOICE

1. Can you see how a refuge city is an image of Jesus? What do you think about that?

   _____
   _____
   _____

2. Have you decided to follow Christ? If so, take a moment to pray with gratitude. If not, how do you feel now about what you've read? And are you willing to say yes to Christ?

   _____
   _____
   _____

3. Do you find yourself running to someone or something else besides God for refuge? Describe.

   _____
   _____
   _____

VERSE FOCUS

For God so loved the world that he gave his one and only Son, that whoever believes in him shall not perish but have eternal life. For God did not send his Son into the world to condemn the world, but to save the world through him. ▸ **John 3:16–17**

WEEK 9
DO NOT FEAR

DAILY READINGS

- Day 1: Deuteronomy 9–12
- Day 2: Deuteronomy 13–16
- Day 3: Deuteronomy 17–20
- Day 4: Deuteronomy 21–24
- Day 5: Deuteronomy 25–28
- **Day 6: Deuteronomy 29–32**
- Day 7: Catch up on any readings you've missed.

"Be strong and courageous. Do not be afraid or terrified because of them, for the Lord your God goes with you." ▶ **Deuteronomy 31: 6**

CHAPTER 31 BEGINS MOSES'S fourth and final speech. These are his last words to the people he led for forty years. The speech begins with a call to Joshua, his next in command, who is taking his place as leader of the Israelites.

Surrounded by everyone, Moses encouraged Joshua with the critical message quoted above. In fact, the chapter uses some variation of this phrase five times.

It was time for the nation to take courage in the Lord and not be afraid. Moses was leaving, and the people could have been afraid to lose the comfort they found in him, but God, not Moses, was caring for them.

It was also an important message to Joshua—he heard it seven different times between Deuteronomy and the book of Joshua. The position of leadership was passing to him so that he would lead millions into a Promised Land, which was no doubt a bit intimidating. He was going to need God, as always.

But Moses did not just issue a call to let go of fear. There was a reason the Israelites didn't need to fear, and that was because God was with them.

When you get worked up about the big year-end exam, you don't have to be afraid of choking, because God is with you. When you get injured playing your favorite sport and have to sit the season out, you don't have to be afraid, because God is with you. When you lose a close friend or family member, you don't have to fear, because God will take care of you.

But let me add, it takes believing in Him and following Him. The people followed God into the Promised Land, and because they were going where He wanted, He was with them. So, take this as your note of confidence: Trust God and He will be with you. And because He's with you, there is nothing to fear.

REWIND AND REJOICE

1. Has there been a time in your life when you were afraid? How did it look on the other side of your fear?

   _____
   _____
   _____

2. Are you afraid of anything now? If so, what is it?

   _____
   _____
   _____

3. How can you give that fear to God and trust Him?

_____

_____

_____

AND I PRAY

Dear Lord,
I know fear can pop up in my life, and I'm so thankful that You know that and put this note in the Bible for me. I don't want to be afraid or worried, and I want to trust You. Will You please go with me and help me not be afraid? I put my trust in You alone, God. Amen.

WEEK 10
DEFINED BY GOD, NOT YOUR PAST

DAILY READINGS

- Day 1: Deuteronomy 33–34
- **Day 2: Joshua 1–4**
- Day 3: Joshua 5–8
- Day 4: Joshua 9–12
- Day 5: Joshua 13–16
- Day 6: Joshua 17–20
- Day 7: Catch up on any readings you've missed.

HAVE YOU EVER DONE something not so great, and it stuck with you? Maybe it made you feel unqualified or not good enough to be part of something. Maybe it was even how you felt coming to God? Well, you're about to see that God has a use for anyone who puts their faith in Him, regardless of their past.

The Book of Joshua is the true story of God's people entering the Promised Land. The first several chapters recount many remarkable and powerful passages that we often go to: God's call to Joshua to be strong and courageous, Rahab hiding the spies, and the Israelites crossing the Jordan. Woven throughout them all is faith—a firm belief in God's care, goodness, and provision. But let's zoom in on Rahab, because she is a powerhouse!

In chapter two, Joshua sent two spies to Jericho to scout out the land, and they found sanctuary in the house of a prostitute named Rahab. Verse 2 says the King of Jericho heard that spies were among them, and it was there that Rahab faced a decision that affected the rest of her life and the lives of others. She could either out the spies or lie and save them. Rahab considered the spies worth saving, even at the expense of the people in her city, so she hid them.

Hebrews 11:31 tells us, *By faith the harlot Rahab did not perish with those who did not believe, when she had received the spies with peace.*

It was by faith that Rahab made this decision. Regardless of her pagan upbringing and immoral profession, Rahab chose to put her trust in this mighty God her people heard about. So she hid the two spies and sent the king's men on a wild goose chase outside the city. Then, after asking the spies to promise her and her family protection, she let down a rope to them for a safe escape.

Long story short, the Israelites took the city but saved Rahab and her family. She, a foreign prostitute, was welcomed into the family of God because of her belief in their God. This means that Rahab seems to be the first Gentile (non-Jewish) convert recorded in Scripture.

It doesn't matter what you've done in your life, how many bad decisions you've made, or whether you never grew up in the church. What matters is your faith in Jesus. Offer that to Him, and God will use you for incredible purposes. There is no mistake so big that God can't forgive it.

REWIND AND REJOICE

1. Do you ever feel unworthy of your relationship with Christ? That's not necessarily a bad thing—none of us are worthy. But what from your past seems to linger?

2. Will you pray right now and share with God what you wrestle with and ask for His divine forgiveness?

3. How is God asking you to be brave today and make a stand for Him?

BIBLE TRUTHS

Rahab ended up marrying a man from the tribe of Judah named Salmon, and they had a son named Boaz, whom we will read about in the book of Ruth. King David and then Joseph, the legal father of Jesus, are her direct descendants. Meaning Rahab is listed in the ancestry of Jesus.

WEEK 11
PEACE OVER FEAR

DAILY READINGS

- Day 1: Joshua 21–24
- Day 2: Judges 1–5
- Day 3: Judges 6–9
- Day 4: Judges 10–13
- Day 5: Judges 14–17
- **Day 6: Judges 18–21**
- Day 7: Catch up on any readings you've missed.

In those days Israel had no king; everyone did as they saw fit.

▸ **Judges 21:25**

JUDGES IS A BOOK rich in history but steeped in sad stories. Israel is now in the Promised Land, Joshua is gone, and the nation has no human leader. They are meant to follow God, but instead they follow their desires and do whatever they want. As a result, lots of people got hurt. The people wandered, God sent an enemy nation to bring them back to Him, they cried out to God, and God raised up a judge to deliver them out of the enemy's hands—a person God would use to temporarily lead the nation.

One such judge was the supernaturally strong Samson, whom God raised to help the people of Israel against the Philistines. From the moment he was born, God and his parents set Samson aside as a Nazarite, which basically meant he was committed to a vow or special dedication to God.

Samson met a girl and, long story short, in chapter 16 she betrayed him, and he was put into prison. One day, when they brought Samson out to taunt him, he used that supernatural strength from God to bring down the building and kill all his enemies.

Judges and Samson show us that doing things that seem right to us but that go against God's way and lack His guidance often lead to bad situations. They also show us that when we lean into our ways and strength, we miss the partnership God wants to have with us. Samson took for granted what God had given him, and he used it for his own benefit.

God has equipped you with gifts and calling for His purposes that will serve others. Seek His plan and use it for His glory. If you're wondering what that plan is, get close to Him. Ask God how He wants to use you for His good plans. Ask Him to provide all you need to accomplish His purposes.

I hope you see, as you progress through this book, the relationship between our closeness with God and His provision.

REWIND AND REJOICE

1. What is your takeaway from this devotional and the idea that doing what seems right to you may also lead to pain?

   _____
   _____
   _____

2. What gifts has God put in you for this season of life?

   _____
   _____
   _____

3. How can you use those gifts to serve Him and others?

   _____
   _____
   _____

LIVE IN LIGHT

1. It helps to talk with people who know you to see what kind of gifting they see in your life. Have some conversations with family, friends, or mentors about what they see in your life that God can use.

2. Find one way to use your gifts this week.

3. In your needs, seek God and note His provision.

WEEK 12
SHELTER UNDER HIS WINGS

DAILY READINGS

- **Day 1: Ruth 1–4**
- Day 2: 1 Samuel 1–4
- Day 3: 1 Samuel 5–8
- Day 4: 1 Samuel 9–12
- Day 5: 1 Samuel 13–17
- Day 6: 1 Samuel 18–20
- Day 7: Catch up on any readings you've missed.

RUTH IS A BEAUTIFUL book that God has used often in my life to encourage my weary heart. When I've been unsure of the path, when I've doubted His working in my life, when I have felt beyond His redeeming love, Ruth reminds me that God is moving and working. And I pray that you too, after reading her story, will feel assured that God cares about all His people, including you. That He is working behind the scenes even when you can't see it. Just like Ruth.

The book of Ruth mentions God a few times, but there are no direct conversations or miraculous events, no dreams or visions, and no prayers recorded. It's about a woman new to the faith embarking on a journey and finding her forever family in God's kingdom.

Like me, you may have wondered if God is at work in your life. In this book, God is subtly at work as He guides two women down a path of restoration and fruitfulness.

Ruth and Naomi both return to a town known as the House of Bread at the beginning of the barley harvest. Coincidence? I think not. An unseen force moved, and these two women saw God do great things that were invisible to their eyes at the time, like bringing them to the right field owned by the right person and taking care of all their needs.

God wants to take care of all of us: the foreigner, the poor, the lonely, the broken, and even those who feel bitter. He wants to be your safe space, offering protection, comfort, and joy. We can see a glimpse of this in the story of Boaz and Ruth. Boaz cared for Ruth in a way that reminds us how God cares for us. He wants us to find peace under His wings.

God also wants to provide for you. When Ruth came back to Naomi from Boaz's field, she didn't have just a little food—she had more than she ever expected. Some believe it could have been enough to last for a whole year.

If you're feeling like you're barely holding on, remember that God has so much more planned for you than just getting by. He wants to fill your life with hope, healing, and His goodness.

If there's one thing we can be sure of, it's that no matter how difficult your season may be, you must believe and trust God to provide. As difficult as times may be, allow your faith to stretch into trusting Him. Without this, your faith will never grow to see the fullness of what God wants to do in your life.

REWIND AND REJOICE

1. How do you see God working behind the scenes in Ruth's life?

2. How does that encourage you and help you see God's work in your own life?

3. What is your big takeaway from the book of Ruth?

VERSE FOCUS

Now to him who is able to do immeasurably more than all we ask or imagine, according to his power that is at work within us, to him be glory in the church and in Christ Jesus throughout all generations, for ever and ever! Amen. ▶ **Ephesians 3:20–21**

WEEK 13
FAITHFULNESS OVER FADS

DAILY READINGS

- Day 1: 1 Samuel 21–24
- Day 2: 1 Samuel 25–27
- **Day 3: 1 Samuel 28–31**
- Day 4: 2 Samuel 1–4
- Day 5: 2 Samuel 5–7
- Day 6: 2 Samuel 8–10
- Day 7: Catch up on any readings you've missed.

FAITHFULNESS—today's unsung hero.

Stories of God delivering someone from terrible circumstances are powerful and moving, but what about the testimony of someone who followed God from a young age? I pray that regardless of what your past looks like, you can start today with a testimony of faithfulness. You'll choose to follow God even when things look bleak, and trust God to carry you through.

What does that look like? It means choosing to trust God no matter what difficult circumstances come your way. It means doing what might be unpopular, such as skipping a party, rejecting a drink, or putting aside peer pressure for the freedom God offers to those who follow Him. I can't promise it will be easy, but I can promise you it will be worth it.

I mentioned already that Joseph is my favorite person in the Bible, but another favorite of mine is Samuel. You know what they have in common? Faithfulness. They are two of the most faithful people in the Bible, which is so refreshing. Yes, it's essential to know about those who fumbled, because it lets us know we are not beyond God's use. Yet, reading about the faithful shows us that steadfastness is possible.

Samuel followed God from a young age; he even learned to hear His voice as a teenager. He was a strong spiritual leader for the nation both before and during the reign of the first king of Israel. Then, when he died, as told in chapter 25, the whole nation gathered to mourn him. What a beautiful picture of his legacy!

I know sometimes when you're young you feel like you have your life ahead of you, and the choices you make now aren't that big a deal. But everything does matter. Every decision you make now impacts your future. What you don't want is to accumulate baggage that carries into that future.

The decisions you make today are important, and the life you choose to live now will echo into eternity. I wish I could do over some things from my past, but I can't. But you have time to do things well. Commit your life to God, walk in His ways, and live a life others will look to and see favor in.

REWIND AND REJOICE

1. What does the story of Samuel's life teach you about faithfulness?

   _____
   _____
   _____

2. Do you feel pressured in an area of your life to compromise or go against what you believe God would want for you?

   _____
   _____
   _____

3. How can you do the right thing now or handle situations like that in the future?

   _____
   _____
   _____

AND I PRAY

Dear Lord,
I want to be a woman of faithfulness. Will You please help me? Sometimes I feel drawn to the things of this world, but my heart is for You. I ask, Holy Spirit, that You enable me to stay faithful and make choices that honor You. I love You and my heart is Yours, Father. Amen.

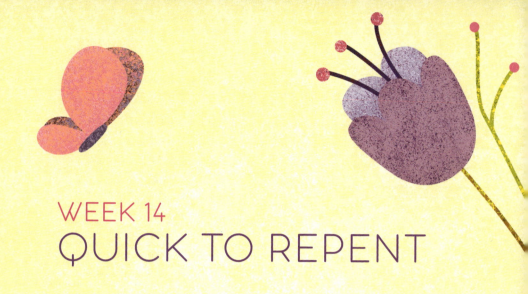

WEEK 14
QUICK TO REPENT

DAILY READINGS

- Day 1: 2 Samuel 11–14
- Day 2: 2 Samuel 15–17
- Day 3: 2 Samuel 18–20
- Day 4: 2 Samuel 21–24
- Day 5: 1 Kings 1–4
- **Day 6: 1 Kings 5–8**
- Day 7: Catch up on any readings you've missed.

HAVE YOU EVER STRUGGLED to talk with God after you've messed up? Sometimes when you've sinned, you feel this fear or shame that tells you to run from God. Today, we're going to see that running *to* God should be the very thing you do.

I didn't do this on purpose, but of course, God knew what He was doing when He led me to put this reading plan together for you. It's so cool, because this week's reading opens with a need for an act of repentance, and it also closes with repentance.

We open with King David, the greatest king of Israel. He was a man after God's own heart (1 Samuel 13:14), and while he made mistakes, his heart was ever tender toward the Lord. In 2 Samuel 11, he made one of the biggest mistakes of his life. He slept with a married woman and had her husband killed. Yes, it's tragic. The thing is, when David was confronted with his sin, as told in the next chapter, he genuinely repented. That's the thing about a heart that is tender toward God—your heart hurts at sin and you learn to quickly make things right with God.

Then we jump to 1 Kings 8 and read a chapter about repentance and how it leads to restoration. Solomon, David's son and heir to the throne, blessed the new temple. And in this speech, Solomon made a series of statements about sin, followed by confession. They were if/then statements—"if" the people did this, "then" God would do this. It's incredible to see the correlation. It again speaks to repentance leading to restoration.

This theme of repentance in David's life has encouraged me over the years. I tend to be stubborn, and in my youth I would deny wrongdoing. But now I try to practice quick repentance. When I mess up, I go right to God and make it right—not as a performance but because I truly want to repair what I've done.

I hope these readings do the same for you. Be quick to repent, sweet sister in Christ. Know the wrong you've done, share with God how sorry you are, and ask for His forgiveness. It's such a freeing and beautiful process.

REWIND AND REJOICE

1. How many if/then statements do you count in 1 Kings 8, and which one sticks out the most to you? Why?

   _____
   _____
   _____

2. Is there something you've been holding back from God? He already knows, but He wants you to come to Him.

   _____
   _____
   _____

3. What would you like to express to God in the light of this confession?

   _____
   _____
   _____

BIBLE TRUTHS

The king who came before David, Saul, messed up a lot, too. And as a result, God took his kingdom away from him. The difference between Saul and David is that David was quick to repent because he understood that God is gracious. In contrast, Saul didn't grasp God's grace and stubbornly held on to his sins.

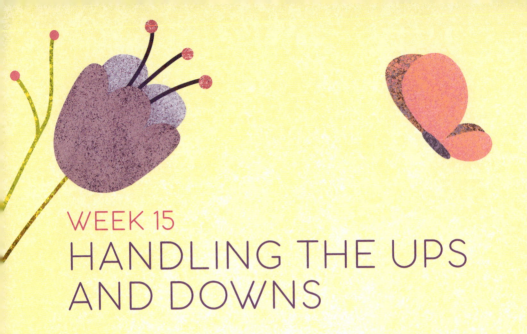

WEEK 15
HANDLING THE UPS AND DOWNS

DAILY READINGS

- Day 1: 1 Kings 9–12
- Day 2: 1 Kings 13–16
- **Day 3: 1 Kings 17–19**
- Day 4: 1 Kings 20–22
- Day 5: 2 Kings 1–4
- Day 6: 2 Kings 5–8
- Day 7: Catch up on any readings you've missed.

THE YEAR I GRADUATED from my discipleship program was definitely the *best* year of my life up until that point—we're talking twenty years—and still stands as a banner year for me. I felt like I was on top of the mountain, even in those hard pockets. But then I came off that mountain and hit a spiritual low.

Have you ever had that feeling? Maybe it was summer camp, and you had a powerful time at the altar, but then you came back home and people in your life didn't seem as excited about your spiritual experience as you felt. Or perhaps you went on a mission trip and felt a call to ministry, but you came back and didn't know what was next or where to start.

Sometimes, we hit spiritual highs and then we come off the mountaintop to something very different, and we get discouraged. We forget what God has done.

Elijah, the prophet, experienced a similar roller coaster of emotions, in 1 Kings 18–19. God used him to point a wandering nation back toward Him in a dramatic display in which fire was called down from the sky. People saw firsthand that Elijah served the one true God while the Baal prophets followed a false god.

But then things shifted for Elijah. Maybe he hoped the evil king and queen would repent. They didn't, and the queen threatened Elijah's life. So he ran away into the desert, where he experienced a deep depression. It was so bad he wanted to die. But God encouraged Elijah at his lowest point, and he went on to have the most beautiful moment with God on a mountaintop, being whispered to and intimately met by God.

What do you do during the ups and downs? Elijah's life shows us a few things we can adopt for ourselves.

1. Stay connected to God and talk to Him through the good and bad.

2. Give Him glory in every season.

3. Take time to rest and focus on God if you feel like you don't have much to give right now.

If you can learn how to navigate the ups and downs, you may not have to wrestle quite as hard. And don't forget to give God praise on the mountain and seek His quiet voice when you are uncertain.

REWIND AND REJOICE

1. Have you ever gone from the mountaintop to the desert? Describe that experience.

2. What encourages you to press in when you don't see God moving or hear His voice?

3. Have you ever sensed that God was speaking to you? Did you brush it off or did you try to listen? Either way, did you learn anything from that moment?

LIVE IN LIGHT

1. Note Elijah's experience on the mountain when God speaks to him in a whisper. How can you quiet your own life so you can hear God's whisper?

2. During your low points, seek God for His presence and voice.

3. Be bold this week in your faith, and show the people around you that God is real and loves them.

WEEK 16
YOUR FIRST FOCUS

DAILY READINGS

- Day 1: 2 Kings 9–12
- Day 2: 2 Kings 13–16
- **Day 3: 2 Kings 17–19**
- Day 4: 2 Kings 20–22
- Day 5: 2 Kings 23–25
- Day 6: 1 Chronicles 1–4
- Day 7: Catch up on any readings you've missed.

All this took place because the Israelites had sinned against the Lord their God ... They worshiped other gods. ▸ **2 Kings 17:7**

THERE'S THIS PRINCIPLE THAT bad choices lead to bad results, while good choices lead to good results. And while that's true, as we see here, it's also not enough. If you're wondering what is, keep reading!

The rest of 2 Kings tells a series of stories about the kings of Israel and Judah. These nations were once a single kingdom, but after the reign of Solomon, the Northern Kingdom became Israel, and the Southern Kingdom, where Jerusalem was, became Judah.

Israel, to the north, always had a bad king. In fact, their kings were noted for being evil and doing their own thing, refusing to seek God. Judah, on the other hand, had some good kings. They weren't perfect, but some did choose to follow the Law.

You'll see that it didn't end well for those who rejected God. They usually died tragically, had the kingdom taken away from their family, or faced terrible opposition. Yet, for those who followed God, there was grace and favor. That doesn't mean things were easy, but God cared for the king and the nation who sought Him.

The reality is that those who reject God will struggle without grace in their life and find eternal judgment at the end. For those who seek God, there's favor and an eternal reward.

You are not too young to understand the natural consequences of sin and to see that a life well lived is one that honors God. The enemy knows this well, and he wants you to believe it's not a big deal. The enemy wants you to believe that as long as you're a good person and don't do anything "too" bad, you're on your way to the pearly gates. But no one is good enough to get there, not even the relatively good leaders we're reading about in Kings. Only One is good. His name is Jesus, and we need Him alone to bridge the gap.

If I can encourage you with one takeaway this week, it's this: Seek God first. The Bible is clear that when you do, God takes care of everything else. He will help you navigate friendships, boys, school, stress, and so much more. Why not commit to Him and see

Him take the burden from you so you don't have to carry it? Live in and for Him, and there will be a grace that just makes life sweeter.

REWIND AND REJOICE

1. Read about the evil kings this week, and in your journal, note your observations about how the absence of God impacted their lives.

   _____
   _____
   _____

2. In contrast, note observations about the good kings and their walk with God.

   _____
   _____
   _____

3. Where could you use God's help—His grace—this week?

   _____
   _____
   _____

VERSE FOCUS

But seek first his kingdom and his righteousness, and all these things will be given to you as well. ▶ **Matthew 6:33**

WEEK 17
FIND YOUR PEOPLE

DAILY READINGS

- Day 1: 1 Chronicles 5–8
- **Day 2: 1 Chronicles 9–12**
- Day 3: 1 Chronicles 13–16
- Day 4: 1 Chronicles 17–20
- Day 5: 1 Chronicles 21–24
- Day 6: 1 Chronicles 25–29
- Day 7: Catch up on any readings you've missed.

HAVE YOU EVER HEARD, "Show me your friends and I'll show you your future?" Well, I can attest to its truth.

I've had the same best friend, Joanna, since I was fourteen years old, which means we've been in each other's lives for twenty-five years. We met in middle school French class, and after all these years, she is still one of the few people in this world I can really be myself with. We both gave our hearts to Jesus, at the same church and around the same time. We went into the same discipleship program together. I was her maid of honor and today, she and her husband pastor the church my family goes to, and our kids are friends. It's seriously the coolest thing. We get each other because we go *way* back.

One person in the Bible who knew a thing or two about great friends was David. His friendship with Jonathan, Saul's son, was incredible. Jonathan was technically heir to the throne, but he didn't care—he knew God was with David. Jonathan and David were more like brothers than anything else.

Then you have David's mighty men, his inner circle of warriors, who stuck with him through thick and thin. We read about some of them in 1 Chronicles 11. Those men were incredibly important to David. He needed them just as much as they needed him.

But how do you build that inner circle? You have to start with other people who love God, too. That's the most important foundation. Then look for people you can trust, who will stick by your side and who will laugh and celebrate with you.

David had great friends and trusted people around him, and I imagine that if he had not had them, his story would have been different. I know mine would be different without women such as my friend Joanna. People who love God and love us are gold in our lives.

What kind of friends are around you? Are they the kind of girls who will encourage you in the Lord when you're down, love you at your ugliest, and be a faithful friend through the good and bad? Find your own Jonathan and mighty men. I found mine, and they have truly been some of the best blessings in my life. I promise you that if you find yours, you will feel the same.

REWIND AND REJOICE

1. What kind of friendships do you have in your life right now? Do they help you know Jesus better or do they take you further away from Him?

   _____
   _____
   _____

2. Are there aspects of friendship you're missing that you'd like to pray for in a new friend?

   _____
   _____
   _____

3. How can you invest in the friends you have today and help them feel seen?

   _____
   _____
   _____

AND I PRAY

Dear Lord,
I long to have great friends who will stick with me through the good and bad, friends who love You and share the same beliefs I do. I'm thankful for those You have brought into my life, and I pray You will continue to show me the kind of people You want me to be around. I pray for incredible friendships, please, God. Amen.

WEEK 18
STANDING IN GOD WHEN YOU'RE WORRIED

DAILY READINGS

- Day 1: 2 Chronicles 1–4
- Day 2: 2 Chronicles 5–8
- Day 3: 2 Chronicles 9–12
- Day 4: 2 Chronicles 13–16
- **Day 5: 2 Chronicles 17–20**
- Day 6: 2 Chronicles 21–24
- Day 7: Catch up on any readings you've missed.

ABOUT FIVE YEARS AGO, I went through a pretty embarrassing situation at the hands of people I trusted. I felt misunderstood, slandered, and angry. I didn't quite know how to handle the situation, so I stuffed it down, afraid to talk about it with anyone. Have you ever felt like that? Worried after a fight with a friend or embarrassed by a prank your brother pulled? It happens, unfortunately, but the good news is there is some encouragement to hold on to.

In 2 Chronicles 20, King Jehoshaphat of Judah called the people to trust in the Lord to fight a big battle. He said,

Do not be afraid or discouraged because of this vast army. For the battle is not yours, but God's… You will not have to fight this battle. Take up your positions; stand firm and see the deliverance the Lord will give you, Judah and Jerusalem. Do not be afraid; do not be discouraged. Go out to face them tomorrow, and the Lord will be with you. ▸ **(2 Chronicles 20:15, 17)**

I felt nervous and a bit worried in my own situation, but I knew I needed to trust God. Sometimes, facing a situation you don't understand or people who oppose you can be intimidating, maybe even frightening. Perhaps it's stressful and worrisome. I totally get it. It's not a fun place to be. The kingdom of Judah felt it, but you know what? God took care of the situation by defeating their enemies for them. They never even had to fight. And God will do the same for you.

This passage has given me a lot of hope, and I pray it does for you as well. You don't have to stress and worry because God is security. He is hope. He will fight the battles that seem too big. He will defend you against the people who seem to have the upper hand. You must stand and trust the Lord to do what you can't do.

So, if you're in a battle you feel you can't win, and stress and worry seem to take over, take a breath and focus on God. Stand firm in Him and He will be with you.

REWIND AND REJOICE

1. How do the words in 2 Chronicles 20:15–17 encourage you?

   _____
   _____
   _____

2. Are you feeling stressed or worried right now about anything? How do these verses impact the situation?

   _____
   _____
   _____

3. What can you take away from this devotional and passage that will strengthen you for the next battle?

   _____
   _____
   _____

BIBLE TRUTHS

Do you know what happened to Jehoshaphat and the people of Judah? They began to sing and praise God, and the Lord sent a surprise ambush against their enemies. Judah didn't even have to fight. Their enemies killed themselves, and the people of Judah got to walk away with spoils so great they couldn't carry it all.

WEEK 19
FAVOR TO THE HUMBLE

DAILY READINGS

- Day 1: 2 Chronicles 25–28
- Day 2: 2 Chronicles 29–32
- Day 3: 2 Chronicles 33–36
- Day 4: Ezra 1–5
- Day 5: Ezra 6–10
- **Day 6: Nehemiah 1–4**
- Day 7: Catch up on any readings you've missed.

God opposes the proud but shows favor to the humble.

▸ **James 4:5**

SOMETIMES, LIFE PRESENTS A SITUATION that changes everything. It might be where you go to college or whether you choose to take an unpopular stance at school. But one thing is for sure—you must tackle it with humility and with God.

I know I said faithfulness is a great unsung hero, but humility is, too. The world honors us when we are proud, but God honors us when we are humble.

Ezra and Nehemiah are historical books in the Bible that describe the time when the people of God were freed from their exile and allowed to return home. In Ezra, waves of Israelites begin traveling back to rebuild the temple in Jerusalem. In Ezra 8, the people fast and pray for God's help in this great endeavor, and He moves on their behalf.

In Nehemiah, we read about the rebuilding of the wall; without it, the city was left vulnerable. Some people were against the work Nehemiah was leading, but he stood firm.

In contrast, it is noted in Nehemiah 3:5 that while all the Israelites were contributing to the wall, a group of nobles *would not stoop to serve their Lord* (ESV). They felt above the work, and the only thing we know about their lives is their pride.

Moments of great courage or decisiveness will come—how will you engage the moment? In pride, boasting of what you can do or believing you are above the hard work? Or in humility, embracing the work God has called you to do?

In our culture, it takes a lot of courage to stand firm while holding on to humility (meaning, being bold in your faith while surrendering to God to lead you). It goes against the grain. That said, I am so confident—and I hope you will be, too—that God's way is not just the best way but the *only* way.

So, when it comes time to pick a school, can you make that decision with God? Or when someone at school is mocked, will you stand up with them? Surrender your will and preferences to God, and His favor will rest upon you.

REWIND AND REJOICE

1. How would you describe your understanding of pride before and after today's devotional?

   _____
   _____
   _____

2. How would you describe your understanding of humility before and after today's devotional?

   _____
   _____
   _____

3. Which do you think actually takes more strength to show, and why?

   _____
   _____
   _____

LIVE IN LIGHT

1. Find ways this week to respond humbly, maybe with a parent or at school, and note how it affects the situation.

2. How can you take a stand this week for your faith?

WEEK 20
YOU WERE MADE FOR NOW

DAILY READINGS

- Day 1: Nehemiah 5–7
- Day 2: Nehemiah 8–10
- Day 3: Nehemiah 11–13
- **Day 4: Esther 1–4**
- Day 5: Esther 5–7
- Day 6: Esther 8–10
- Day 7: Catch up on any readings you've missed.

YOU WERE MADE FOR this time, sweet girl. You are where God has placed you, whether that's a good or a hard spot, for a very specific purpose, and it's up to you to search out why. Let's look at Proverbs 25:2, which has a beautiful addition to this thought:

It is the glory of God to conceal a matter; to search out a matter is the glory of kings.

This basically means God has it all planned, but it's up to you and me, and to our glory, to find out what this plan is.

Esther was one young woman who had a calling to determine. She was an Israelite living in exile under the Persian king (Persia is modern-day Iran). The king was looking for a wife, and he held what was essentially a grand beauty pageant. He chose Esther as his wife and queen, and that is how this young Hebrew woman entered the palace.

Except, the king didn't know she was in exile, and eventually he made a proclamation against her people. Esther's uncle pleaded with her to do something, and he said the famous words in Esther 4:14: *And who knows but that you have come to your royal position for such a time as this?*

Esther was there, at that place and at that time, for a reason. And maybe it was so she could save her people. How did Esther handle the moment? She declared that if she must perish, she would, but she had to do something. And Esther went on to save her people.

What we learn from Esther, the book and the person, is that God has not made a mistake about your life. You are here for a reason, and there is a purpose for your life. It may not be saving lives, but it could be. Maybe right now it's being a light at your school. Perhaps it's being a light to your own family.

Youth does not disqualify you from God's plans. And I encourage you to make the most of the plans God has for you.

REWIND AND REJOICE

1. What about the life of Esther inspires you?

   _____
   _____
   _____

2. Is it easy or hard for you to believe that you are made for this time and place? Do you feel overlooked because of your age? How does this make you feel and how does this passage encourage you?

   _____
   _____
   _____

3. Is God stirring in your heart something that you can act on today?

   _____
   _____
   _____

VERSE FOCUS

"And if I perish, I perish." ▸ **Esther 4:16**

WEEK 21
WISDOM FOR YOUR SUFFERING

DAILY READINGS

- **Day 1: Job 1–5**
- Day 2: Job 6–9
- Day 3: Job 10–13
- Day 4: Job 14–17
- Day 5: Job 18–21
- Day 6: Job 22–24
- Day 7: Catch up on any readings you've missed.

I'M GOING TO BE up-front with you: Job is a big book with a lot of feeling and a lot of suffering. Because of this, it's not exactly the easiest book to read, but I promise you it is rich in wisdom. And that's really the crux of its value—it gives great insight into how we should suffer, because suffering does come to us all.

It's about a man named Job who had a large family, great wealth, and a lot of respect from others. But most important, he loved God. One day, Satan asked God to allow him to bring disaster to Job, with the assumption that Job loved God only because God blessed him. So, God allowed Satan to test Job's faith. Job lost every one of his children and all his wealth in one day. It was tragic and sobering.

What we find in Job is largely a series of conversations Job had with three of his friends after this tragedy. The friends speak in three rounds, each ending with Job's reply. They believe that Job must have had sin in him to have that kind of suffering. Yet Job 1:22 tells us, *In all this, Job did not sin by charging God with wrongdoing.* Job stayed faithful to God.

I want to note Job's response. We already saw that Job did not sin in his suffering—he did not curse God or walk away from his faith. He remained steadfast. He didn't say God was bad or wrong; he didn't claim God was tempting him to sin. He knew God could be trusted.

But also, I want you to consider the question I've wrestled with in Job: How does someone get to the point where they lose everything and not blame God? I mean, the guy said in 1:21: *Naked I came from my mother's womb, and naked I will depart. The Lord gave and the Lord has taken away; may the name of the Lord be praised.* Wow, what a testimony!

And then, in chapter 20, verses 20 and 26, he says that essentially all he has left is the skin on his bones, but even when that was gone, he would still praise God.

WISDOM FOR YOUR SUFFERING   75

This book will confront your assumptions, insecurities, and fears about suffering. It will beg you to ask yourself if you, too, could remain faithful like Job while in great pain. May I encourage you? Please don't give up when it gets hard. Don't walk away when you feel the pain. Lean into God and trust Him to take care of you.

REWIND AND REJOICE

1. Does Job's suffering change or challenge your understanding of God? If so, how?

   _____
   _____
   _____

2. What are your thoughts about Job's response to his suffering? How does it encourage you to think about your own pain?

   _____
   _____
   _____

3. After you have finished this week's readings, note in your journal what stood out to you the most.

   _____
   _____
   _____

AND I PRAY

Dear Lord,
I know suffering is part of life, and that seems scary sometimes. But I want to be like Job when the hurt comes. I want to trust You and remain faithful. Will You please help me, God, to weather the storms well? And to point others to You in the pain. Amen.

WEEK 22
PEACE IN A PERSON

DAILY READINGS

- [ ] Day 1: Job 25–28
- [ ] Day 2: Job 29–32
- [ ] Day 3: Job 33–36
- [x] **Day 4: Job 37–39**
- [ ] Day 5: Job 40–42
- [ ] Day 6: Psalms 1–5
- [ ] Day 7: Catch up on any readings you've missed.

IN HIGH SCHOOL, I experienced a lot of pain, both physically and emotionally. I held so much anger and bitterness in from past abuse that I ended up depressed and literally bent over in pain from a near ulcer. I had a lot of questions about what I was going through and what I faced, but I didn't know where to direct them. So I just stayed angry.

Then I decided to give my life to Jesus, and much of that pain and anger went away. But that didn't mean I never again had questions. To this day, I still have questions about the pain in my life. But I know *who* to direct them to and *how*, much like Job did.

In the second half of this book, we see Job ask God all the hard questions but find peace in not knowing. Maybe you've asked the same questions. Perhaps you've wrestled to find peace when things hurt. God has something to say to you for those moments.

In chapters 38–41, God posed seventy questions to Job. For example, in chapter 38: 4–7, God asks:

Where were you when I laid the earth's foundation? Tell me, if you understand. Who marked off its dimensions? Surely you know! Who stretched a measuring line across it? On what were its footings set, or who laid its cornerstone—while the morning stars sang together and all the angels shouted for joy?

God's questions to Job were technically meant to be unanswered, showing Job that he couldn't demand answers from God. But thinking that God's appearance was only to scold Job is a mistake. God showed up for Job. Job's biggest hardship was feeling abandoned by God, and now he knew he wasn't abandoned, because God spoke to him. While God's greatness made Job feel small, he was comforted just knowing God was with him again.

The great takeaway I leave with you is this: Peace is found not in an answer but in a person. And that person is Christ. In your pain, you can wrestle out your questions with God—He is a safe place. Ultimately, your peace won't come from knowing why but who. You will have peace in the pain because Jesus is the answer.

REWIND AND REJOICE

1. Have your thoughts about suffering shifted as you've read through Job?

   _____
   _____
   _____

2. What do you think about God's response to Job and Job's response to Him?

   _____
   _____
   _____

3. How can you find your peace in God?

   _____
   _____
   _____

BIBLE TRUTHS

You know what's really cool? God restored Job's family and fortune. God not only blessed Job, but the Bible also says God blessed him more in the aftermath than He had before. Job's life ended, as the Scripture notes, when he was an old man full of days, which is a way of saying he was satisfied with this life. Wow, what a beautiful ending to such a challenging and emotional book.

WEEK 23
DIRECTING YOUR THOUGHTS

DAILY READINGS

- Day 1: Psalms 6–9
- Day 2: Psalms 10–15
- Day 3: Psalms 16–18
- **Day 4: Psalms 19–22**
- Day 5: Psalms 23–27
- Day 6: Psalms 28–31
- Day 7: Catch up on any readings you've missed.

I LOVE THE BOOK of Psalms. It's probably the book I return to the most because it's so relatable and rich in the beautiful expression of a human heart that maintains steady hope in God.

What you're going to see, though, is a steady focus on God in the good and the bad. And may it show you that no matter what you go through, you must look to God, because He wants to share the ups and downs with you.

The Book of Psalms is a collection of poems and songs written during a period that began with Moses and stretched through Israel's captivity. It's a beautiful book containing declarations of God's goodness and faithfulness, even during times of trial and suffering.

One thing you'll notice about the psalms is that while they often focus on pain and grief, the authors always see that suffering through hope in God. These writers focus on God, and that meditation carries them through life's challenges.

Take Psalm 19—it echoes this theme. The very last verse shares the writer's heart to keep God central: *May these words of my mouth and this meditation of my heart be pleasing in your sight, Lord, my Rock and my Redeemer.*

The psalmist sees that it's not hard to focus on God because God constantly reveals Himself to us. In this chapter, note that there is a natural revelation of God in verses 1–6 and a special revelation in verses 7–14.

What I mean by "natural" is that you can look at the sky and creation, and it all reveals a Divine work behind it. "Special" revelation is His word; through the Bible, God reveals to you and me incredible insight into who He is and what He is about.

Maybe you look up and feel moved to worship Him. Or when you're hurting, you turn to His Word for comfort. God has something for you no matter what you are going through.

All this to say, there is no better place to direct your thoughts than toward God. He is faithful, just, merciful, and wise, and He provides everything you need to live. If you set your mind on Him rather than the material things of this world, you will find exactly what you need to sustain you through the good and the bad.

If you hurt, filter that hurt through Him. If you're unsure, bring those questions to God. When you meditate on or think about His Word daily, you are better equipped to navigate whatever comes your way.

REWIND AND REJOICE

1. If you were to go through something awful, and maybe you are now, how would you approach that hurt? Through God or through something you learned as a way to deal with pain? Describe that focus.

   _____
   _____
   _____
   _____

2. Write out your favorite verse from Psalm 19 that you can turn to for encouragement.

   _____
   _____
   _____
   _____

3. How would you define the difference between God's natural revelation and His special revelation, and how can you appreciate both?

_____

_____

_____

_____

LIVE IN LIGHT

1. I have several verses in Psalm 19 memorized because they remind me of God's faithfulness when I need it most. Memorize one verse this week that you can carry with you.

2. Note God's natural revelation—appreciate the sunset or something beautiful you see in creation and thank God.

WEEK 24
LEADING YOUR EMOTIONS

DAILY READINGS

- Day 1: Psalms 32–34
- Day 2: Psalms 35–37
- Day 3: Psalms 38–40
- **Day 4: Psalms 41–44**
- Day 5: Psalms 45–49
- Day 6: Psalms 50–53
- Day 7: Catch up on any readings you've missed.

DO YOU EVER LET your emotions brew inside for too long? I know I sometimes do. And then I begin letting my emotions lead my choices and influence how I see situations. Pre-Christian Brittany would have let those emotions build until they exploded. Post-salvation Brittany has learned to lead her emotions, not the other way around. If you tend to do the same, you know it's not always easy, is it? May today provide some relief and help for you.

Psalm 42 is my favorite psalm because it's beautiful and cuts to the human heart. Things were not going well for the writer; some people thought he may have been depressed. He was wrestling with his feelings of deep sadness, but he also knew he couldn't stay in that mindset. So what did he do? He chose to focus on his need for God and put all his hope and trust in Him.

Maybe you don't feel like praying and calling out to Him, but that is the very thing you must do. Look, the psalmist understands pain but he also understood the importance of seeking God first, despite how he felt. If you and I allow our emotions to lead us, we'll rarely feel like getting hold of ourselves, so that will not work if we want to live a life with God.

Here are four tips to help you work through your feelings.

1. Get God's Word into you to feed your soul.

2. Pray.

3. See the situation through a lens of hope anchored in God, rather than through the discouragement of this world.

4. Act as Jesus would in that situation.

You are in charge of your feelings, not the other way around. But it all starts with a desperation for one thing: God.

Let me ask you: Are you desperate for more of God? So desperate that you'll do anything to satisfy that thirst?

I want to encourage you today to pull away, find a quiet spot without distraction, and cry out to Him from your desperation. His presence will be like refreshing water, satisfying your needs.

REWIND AND REJOICE

1. The writer of Psalm 42 redirected his feelings because he was desperate for God above anything else (see verses 1-2). What inspires you about those two verses?

   _____
   _____
   _____

2. What does it look like for you to get hold of your emotions? Where are you most stretched in the four tips I gave?

   _____
   _____
   _____

3. How do you need God's help today?

   _____
   _____
   _____

VERSE FOCUS

"Why, my soul, are you downcast? Why so disturbed within me? Put your hope in God, for I will yet praise him, my Savior and my God." ▶ **Psalm 42:11**

WEEK 25
WHY THINGS CAN GET HARD

DAILY READINGS

- Day 1: Psalms 54–58
- Day 2: Psalms 59–63
- **Day 3: Psalms 64–68**
- Day 4: Psalms 69–71
- Day 5: Psalms 72–75
- Day 6: Psalms 76–78
- Day 7: Catch up on any readings you've missed.

HAVE YOU EVER BEEN through something really hard and thought, "Why am I going through this trouble and pain?"

In high school I kept a diary and wrote about what I was going through. In my sophomore year, I was struggling to find my footing, so I wrote about my frustrations with peers and situations. One day, I left my diary in my backpack on a trip and, somehow, one of the girls got hold of it and started reading it. News quickly spread to my friends about what I wrote, and it caused some issues.

I wasn't a believer yet, but this happened mere months before I met Jesus. It was a season of drama, depression, and struggles, culminating in the hardest year of my life up until that point. But I look back now and see how all of that was meant to bring me to the place where I would be desperate for Jesus when hearing the Gospel.

In Psalm 66:11–12, the writer shares a stirring look at trials and suffering.

For you, God, tested us; you refined us like silver. You brought us into prison and laid burdens on our backs. You let people ride over our heads; we went through fire and water, but you brought us to a place of abundance.

Trials come to test our faith and point us to Jesus. It's in the hard times that we see God's miracle-working power. The psalmist shared that God tested the people to refine them and purify their hearts. The trial was framed with burden and fire, but it led to freedom and endurance. Similarly, tough seasons are meant to pull out the unlovely in you and refine you into someone becoming more like Christ. God is doing something good in the bad.

Maybe you're at odds with some girls at school right now, or your family is going through something unexpected and hard, or perhaps you feel lost and hurt like I did my sophomore year. Remember that it's for a season and for a purpose. God uses the fire to pull out the bad and to make us more like Him. It hurts, but it's worth it.

REWIND AND REJOICE

1. Have you ever been through something hard, but looking back, you can see God was doing something good through the test? Share that experience below.

   _____
   _____
   _____

2. The psalmist wrote that he cried out to God and brought offerings. In your own trial, what would it look like to seek God?

   _____
   _____
   _____

3. What speaks to you from Psalm 66?

   _____
   _____
   _____

AND I PRAY

Dear Lord,
Hard things happen, and sometimes I wrestle with the why. But instead of focusing on the why and the circumstances, I really want to focus on You. Will you please help me, God, to trust You with my trials and believe You are working out something good? Thank you for your strength and help to do what I can't do on my own. Amen.

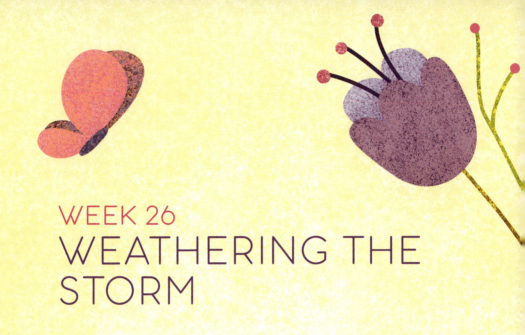

WEEK 26
WEATHERING THE STORM

DAILY READINGS

- Day 1: Psalms 79–83
- Day 2: Psalms 84–88
- **Day 3: Psalms 89–93**
- Day 4: Psalms 94–98
- Day 5: Psalms 99–103
- Day 6: Psalms 104–106
- Day 7: Catch up on any readings you've missed.

IF I WERE TO tell you that it's a compliment to be compared to a tree, what would you think? Doesn't seem like much of a compliment, does it? Well, let me explain.

In Psalm 92:7, we get a picture contrasting an evil person and a righteous person:

Though the wicked spring up like grass and all evildoers flourish, they will be destroyed forever.

Evil is like grass that sprouts quickly but dies just as fast. Evil may seem to flourish, but it's only temporary. Evil are the people who have chosen to follow the desires of their hearts and the world. They may even seem "good" and have success, but it's not enough to be good, and success is not forever.

The righteous, on the other hand, are like palm trees and cedars. These are the people who have chosen to put God first and live a life that honors Him. And this is where things get fascinating.

Palm trees grow in the desert, a climate hard to thrive in. Their roots go deep to find water, so even in harsh conditions, the tree can flourish. Palm trees have uniquely flexible trunks that allow them to bend rather than break during even the strongest storm.

Cedars are also remarkable. The ones in Lebanon can grow up to 120 feet high, and they are resilient to insects. Cedar is often used in buildings because of its durability.

So, what does that have to do with you? Well, that's the kind of character one develops as a result of choosing God. Through His work, you can be made strong, durable, resilient, and built to weather the storm. You don't have to break except before Jesus. You don't have to give up beyond the extent of giving it all to Him. And, ultimately, beyond this life, there is reassurance that you will flourish if you are in Christ.

But again, it comes down to whom you choose to follow and who you choose to be. Will you be driven by the pressures and desires of this world, or will you be a woman of God, following Him and Him alone?

REWIND AND REJOICE

1. What about palm trees and cedars is interesting to you, and how does that apply to a righteous life?

   _____
   _____
   _____

2. We are halfway through this journey together and we've learned a lot about living a holy and righteous life. What has resonated most with you?

   _____
   _____
   _____

3. What choices could you make this week to align yourself more closely with a life totally devoted to God?

   _____
   _____
   _____

BIBLE TRUTHS

While on this theme of plants, let's chat about John 15 and abiding in Christ. It's a beautiful allegory for staying planted in Christ and for the pruning process. We connect ourselves to Jesus, and the Father is the vinedresser who cuts away the unnecessary from our lives. It may hurt and it may mean sacrifice, but it's always worth the process.

WEEK 27
GOING TO GOD OUT OF DESIRE

DAILY READINGS

- Day 1: Psalms 107–110
- Day 2: Psalms 111–118
- Day 3: Psalms 119
- Day 4: Psalms 120–126
- **Day 5: Psalms 127–132**
- Day 6: Psalms 133–138
- Day 7: Catch up on any readings you've missed.

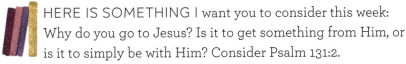 HERE IS SOMETHING I want you to consider this week: Why do you go to Jesus? Is it to get something from Him, or is it to simply be with Him? Consider Psalm 131:2.

I am like a weaned child with its mother; like a weaned child I am content.

Initially, a child wants their mother for food, security, and warmth. But a child weaned is one who longs for their mother's love and relationship.

We see in Psalm 131 that King David found that beautiful and sweet spot of contentment where he chose to go to God because he wanted Him. He desired the peace of a child, so content in its mother's arms that nothing else mattered. Not craving something temporary but craving something meaningful.

Just before those words, David rejects pride and selfish ambition. Indeed, contentment cannot thrive when either persists. The person who lifts up their eyes thinks they have no need for someone else to sustain them. They find everything they need is in themselves, so why would they crave relationship?

In a relationship with God, you don't think of yourself too highly because you recognize that only Jesus is good. And it's with Him you find the peace that surpasses all understanding (Philippians 4:7). You won't find this through acceptance by your peers at school, or achieving perfect grades, or zoning out through drugs or technology. Remember, peace is a person. When you get into His presence, it's beautiful. It's just about being with Him. Not about getting anything, but just being with your Creator and friend.

So, I pray *Psalm 133:2* over your life today: that you would seek God for relationship above all else. It's not wrong to ask God for things; you definitely should. But if your relationship with God is primarily about asking, you will miss the point of the relationship altogether. Put aside your pride and self-pursuits, and seek intimacy with God. There's no greater joy and contentment than that.

REWIND AND REJOICE

1. Would you say you primarily go to God for something you need or simply because you want to? There is no wrong answer. This question is not meant to shame you, but simply to assess your relationship with God right now.

2. How would you describe the correlation between pride and the desire David had for God?

3. Has pride in any form contributed to a distance from God?

LIVE IN LIGHT

1. Spend time each day this week when you don't ask God for anything, but simply enjoy His presence.
2. Think about how you can take everyday tasks like cleaning or playing a sport and commit that time or practice to Christ.

WEEK 28
LIVING WISELY

DAILY READINGS

- Day 1: Psalms 139–144
- Day 2: Psalms 145–150
- **Day 3: Proverbs 1–4**
- Day 4: Proverbs 5–9
- Day 5: Proverbs 10–14
- Day 6: Proverbs 15–19
- Day 7: Catch up on any readings you've missed.

PROVERBS IS A BOOK meant to teach you how to live a wise life. And as we begin it, I want to hold up a passage that beautifully sums up the heart of the book, Proverbs 1:2-3: *For gaining wisdom and instruction; for understanding words of insight; for receiving instruction in prudent behavior, doing what is right and just and fair.*

Its purpose is to give people principles and instructions for living—specifically, living in a way that pleases God. It covers areas such as money, marriage, parenting, friendships, emotions, honesty, work ethic, and much more. It's a gift to humanity in how to navigate all areas of our lives.

If you're wondering if it's worth reading, I can confidently say it is. There may not be a more practical book for living.

Understanding its treasure will likely take a lifetime, but it's a journey worth taking. The question is: Where do you start? The answer is: Fear God (Proverbs 1:7). Take a humble posture, realize you don't have it all figured out, and acknowledge that God is the ultimate source of wisdom.

Then, give everything you have to finding wisdom (Proverbs 4:7). Wisdom has a cost, but it's valuable and worth spending a lifetime searching for. The trouble is, we're often too busy searching for other things: relationships, success, identity, acceptance, and more. But those things will leave you feeling empty.

Solomon, who wrote most of the proverbs, had everything he wanted. What we are seeking, he had. And you know what? In the book of Ecclesiastes, he says it was all "meaningless." All those things he spent a lifetime obtaining left him empty. So, when he tells us in Proverbs to devote everything we have to wisdom, we should take note.

Here are four practices that will help you grow in wisdom.

1. **Read the Bible every day.** Invest your time in gaining godly wisdom from God's Word, and you'll notice a natural grace in your life as it guides you.

2. **Pray as much as you can.** The key is to sit in God's presence with ears open to listen and conversation on your heart.

3. **Get community and a mentor.** Surround yourself with people who can sharpen you.

4. **Practice what you're learning.** What value is gaining understanding if you don't live it?

The book of Proverbs is full of principles and truths for a life well lived. If you follow them, they will guide you, protect you, and fill your life with His wisdom.

REWIND AND REJOICE

1. What are your initial thoughts about or definitions of wisdom?

   _____

   _____

   _____

2. Does it seem like something meant only for those who are older, or is it accessible to younger people as well? Why or why not?

   _____

   _____

   _____

3. Of the four practices given to get wisdom, which do you need to focus on most and implement in your life?

_____

_____

_____

VERSE FOCUS

The beginning of wisdom is this: Get wisdom. Though it cost all you have, get understanding. Cherish her, and she will exalt you; embrace her, and she will honor you. She will give you a garland to grace your head and present you with a glorious crown.

▶ **Proverbs 4:7–9**

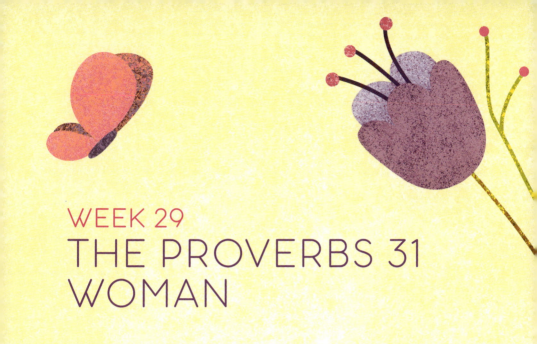

WEEK 29
THE PROVERBS 31 WOMAN

DAILY READINGS

- Day 1: Proverbs 20–24
- Day 2: Proverbs 25–29
- **Day 3: Proverbs 30–31**
- Day 4: Ecclesiastes 1–4
- Day 5: Ecclesiastes 5–8
- Day 6: Song of Solomon 1–8
- Day 7: Catch up on any readings you've missed.

FINALLY, IT'S TIME TO discuss the woman in Proverbs 31. I'm so excited to share her with you. This is the most detailed picture in the Bible of the kind of woman God desires His daughters to resemble.

I get that this woman is older and where she is in her life may feel far down the road from where you're at now, but it's really not that far away, and she is someone you can be *today*. I wish I had started implementing some of her wisdom as a teen so I could have built on it as I grew into my profession and started a family.

This woman was a devoted wife, a nurturing mother, and a wise household manager. Her qualities inspired admiration and respect, serving as an example of strength and grace. She applied herself to gain wisdom and live out that wisdom.

She was competent (v. 10), brought constant and consistent good to the people in her life (v. 11), worked hard (v. 15), gave her best in whatever she produced (v. 18), helped those in need (v. 20), prepared for the future (v. 21), and opened her mouth and taught (v. 26). Opening your mouth indicates thoughtful speech, and teaching on the tongue speaks to something more spontaneous. In season and out of season, the woman was enriched in wisdom and speech.

As a natural result of such living, the woman we examine here would be respected by others and would receive an eternal reward from God (v. 31).

Again, she may seem like the kind of person you will *eventually* become, but this doesn't mean you can't begin laying the foundation now. Find things about her you can begin to take for yourself in your youth. Maybe it's the wisdom about building the future that God desires for you or making choices that will lead to this kind of lifestyle.

Proverbs 31 is a heartfelt tribute to the virtuous woman, a testament to the enduring influence of wisdom, and a celebration of the qualities of strength, dignity, and compassion. It is a call for us, as daughters of the Most High King, to consider and embrace. To devote ourselves to a life to learning and pay the high cost of gaining that knowledge. Being a woman of such valor may seem intimidating, but it's not meant to discourage.

It is wisdom in action for every woman.

REWIND AND REJOICE

1. What are your initial thoughts about this kind of woman?

2. What do you want to take from her today and start weaving into your life?

3. How does she inspire you? Or are there women in your life who model wisdom that inspires you?

AND I PRAY

Dear Lord,
I'm so thankful You've given Scripture an example of the kind of woman who reflects the character of Christ. I truly want to be this kind of woman, like Your Son. Please help me to grow and flourish as Your daughter and be a light to those around me. Amen.

WEEK 30
LOVE IN THE BIBLE

DAILY READINGS

- **Day 1: Song of Solomon 9–12**
- Day 2: Isaiah 1–4
- Day 3: Isaiah 5–8
- Day 4: Isaiah 9–12
- Day 5: Isaiah 13–17
- Day 6: Isaiah 18–22
- Day 7: Catch up on any readings you've missed.

THIS WEEK WE'RE TALKING relationships.
Song of Solomon is a truly moving book you will be able to turn to rather than turning to the world to figure out dating and marriage. It teaches us about love and navigating a relationship. In this book, Solomon is a young man who falls in love with a woman and takes her as his wife. They have a sweet courtship that leads to marriage, but then they eventually wrestle with disagreements. This book covers the ups and downs, the best and worst, of a typical relationship. And within its pages we learn much about loving another.

The first three chapters share a beautiful account of two people falling in love. We learn endearing qualities about the woman, such as her great character (1:3), that she was a hard worker, and that she was a generous person who served others (1:6).

Solomon, in return, was someone proud of her and protected her (2:4). They respected each other, were open (2:14), and trusted each other (2:16). Their example shows us the attributes to look for in a partner and provides guidance on how to navigate a romantic relationship.

The two were married and joined together as one (3:11). They had a love for each other, passion, and open communication. You will find several verses regarding romantic love and physical desire within the bonds of marriage.

In chapter five, the couple fight. She fears losing him, they experience some conflict, and she locks him out of the room. After he tries to get in but can't, he leaves, and she goes out to find him. They eventually reconcile and reunite in their love for each other.

But what does this mean for you, a teenage girl on the cusp of adulthood and relationships?

Well, I'll lead with Song of Solomon 8:4: *Daughters of Jerusalem, I charge you: Do not arouse or awaken love until it so desires.*

I understand the desire and pressure to date, but I really want to encourage you to seek God first and wait for the right time. There's no rush. It's better to wait for the kind of person who loves God and respects you. But even then, I would suggest you look only for a godly man. I didn't date until my twenties, and it was one of the best decisions I made. Guard your heart, sweet girl. It's incredibly valuable.

REWIND AND REJOICE

1. What kind of person do you think God intends for you to date?

2. Also, what kind of woman do you think God desires you to be?

3. We are encouraged to wait on love until the right time. From what you've read in the Bible so far, and pulling from the first two questions, how would Scripture define the right time and situation?

BIBLE TRUTHS

Unfortunately, we know from other books that Solomon had hundreds of wives and concubines. He got lost and strayed, from both God and his wife. In Ecclesiastes 2:10–11, Solomon shares these stirring words: *And whatever my eyes desired I did not keep from them. I kept my heart from no pleasure… Then I considered all that my hands had done…and behold, all was vanity and a striving after wind* (ESV). Solomon reflected on his life and realized his pursuit of pleasure was ultimately meaningless.

WEEK 31
USING YOUR GIFTS GOD'S WAY

DAILY READINGS

- **Day 1: Isaiah 23–27**
- Day 2: Isaiah 28–31
- Day 3: Isaiah 32–35
- Day 4: Isaiah 36–39
- Day 5: Isaiah 40–42
- Day 6: Isaiah 43–45
- Day 7: Catch up on any readings you've missed.

DO YOU EVER GET ANXIOUS? Maybe feel overly nervous before a test? Or fear people, so you avoid interactions altogether? Maybe you get anxious for no reason because that happens, too. Anxiety hits us all, which is why God talks about it in the Bible.

So, what's the secret? Isaiah sets the stage in chapter 26, verse 3: *You will keep in perfect peace those whose minds are steadfast, because they trust in you.*

When you're anxious, help comes from acknowledging that God is in control over all circumstances. It's trusting Him to work things out for you, even when things aren't looking great or perhaps even seem hopeless. You trust that He is bigger than your problem, and when you do this, that problem loses its power over you and doesn't seem as big.

Philippians echoes this but takes it a bit further, bringing the anxiety to God and focusing on Him: *Do not be anxious about anything, but in every situation, by prayer and petition, with thanksgiving, present your requests to God. And the peace of God, which transcends all understanding, will guard your hearts and your minds in Christ Jesus (4:6-7).*

When you feel anxious, pray and give thanks for the blessings and good you do have in your life. When you do that, God's peace will invade the situation and guard your heart and mind from worry.

The Bible is here to help you, and it is filled with wonderful tools. You must be willing to examine, understand, and put them into practice. The next time you feel anxiety rising inside you, pray for God to help you, and think of all the good He has done in your life. This will help you shift your focus and remind you that you can trust in God. He is bigger than any problem. And that will bring you peace.

REWIND AND REJOICE

1. Are you anxious about something today, or do you find yourself getting anxious over the same thing?

   _____
   _____
   _____

2. Write out the process as you see it for how to work through anxiety.

   _____
   _____
   _____

3. What gives you the most hope for finding peace in anxious moments?

   _____
   _____
   _____

LIVE IN LIGHT

1. Meditate on Philippians 4:6–7 this week.
2. Any time you feel anxiety or nerves growing, pray and give thanks!

WEEK 32
ANOINTED TO DO GOOD WORKS

DAILY READINGS

- Day 1: Isaiah 46–48
- Day 2: Isaiah 49–53
- Day 3: Isaiah 54–58
- **Day 4: Isaiah 59–62**
- Day 5: Isaiah 63–66
- Day 6: Jeremiah 1–4
- Day 7: Catch up on any readings you've missed.

The Spirit of the Sovereign Lord is on me, because the Lord has anointed me. ▶ Isaiah 61:1

ISAIAH IS A GREAT BIG book filled with prophecy, and, at times, it can feel like a lot. God certainly covers a lot with recurring themes of sin, mercy, judgment, and hope. Perhaps one of my favorite chapters in it is Isaiah 61 because it's about God anointing Jesus for good works.

It's a beautiful passage to look at because what we see bestowed upon Jesus is for you and me, too (but we'll get to that in a moment). The Spirit of the Lord is on the Messiah because the Lord has anointed Him, and we see how that is worked out to bless people.

In the Bible, anointing was used in a few ways, but one was as an outward symbol—the priests had oil poured on them, which signified that God's presence and favor were with them. And as Christians, we can be anointed as well. In 1 John 2:20, it says, *But you have an anointing from the Holy One.* So, what does that mean? It's like being filled with and blessed by the Holy Spirit.

Here's the cool part: This anointing isn't just for a select few. It's for all of us who follow Jesus. We already have it, but it's something we can grow into more.

But this anointing isn't for yourself. It's so that you can overflow onto others and be a blessing. With this kind of anointing and power, God will use you to bring good news to the poor, heal the brokenhearted, and free those who feel trapped. And you'll get to see God give beauty where there were ashes, gladness where there was mourning, and praise where there was a faint spirit. How incredible to be part of something like that!

You are called on to be a light, to shine in your unique way. Others will see how God has blessed you and will recognize His love through you. Even when you feel insignificant, remember that God has a special plan for your life. He will use your story to bless others.

Will you become more open and responsive to this incredible gift from God? Embrace this call to minister to a hurting world through His Spirit and see how it can change the world.

REWIND AND REJOICE

1. What do you think about the act and the symbol of anointing, both in this chapter and in your life today?

2. Can you see how Jesus fulfilled Isaiah 61? How?

3. How does this passage inspire you to live?

VERSE FOCUS

Jesus returned to Galilee in the power of the Spirit… He stood up to read, and the scroll of the prophet Isaiah was handed to him. Unrolling it, he found the place where it is written: "The Spirit of the Lord is on me…" Then he rolled up the scroll, gave it back to the attendant and sat down. The eyes of everyone in the synagogue were fastened on him. He began by saying to them, "Today this scripture is fulfilled in your hearing." ▸ **Luke 4:14–20**

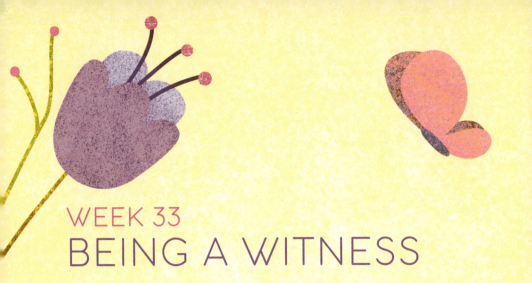

WEEK 33
BEING A WITNESS

DAILY READINGS

- Day 1: Jeremiah 5–8
- Day 2: Jeremiah 9–12
- Day 3: Jeremiah 13–16
- **Day 4: Jeremiah 17–20**
- Day 5: Jeremiah 21–24
- Day 6: Jeremiah 25–28
- Day 7: Catch up on any readings you've missed.

HAVE YOU EVER SHARED the Gospel with someone and they prayed the prayer of salvation? I still remember when I led someone to the Lord for the first time. I shared with her my love of Jesus, and right there, while I held her hands, she prayed for God to save her. I'll never forget that moment.

I haven't always been great at witnessing, and I still don't have it all figured out. But I do know that I never want to be too busy not to tell someone about Christ.

Everything in Jeremiah and the Bible as a whole points to Christ. In Jeremiah 20:9 there is this urgency that can't be ignored.

But if I say, "I will not mention his word or speak anymore in his name," his word is in my heart like a fire, a fire shut up in my bones. I am weary of holding it in; indeed, I cannot.

Jeremiah, the prophet, was ridiculed for declaring the word of God, but that didn't keep him silent. He compared his need to proclaim God to a fire in his bones, just bursting to get out. He couldn't contain it even if he wanted to.

As a believer, you are called to tell people about Jesus—this is called "witnessing." It's talking about Christ and what he has done (and wants to do for each person). A witness is something we are naturally as we live out our lives for Christ. Our natural love and commitment to Him should shine forth and point people to God.

Being an effective witness begins with living a life that naturally draws others to want to learn more. It's also sharing your testimony, talking about Christ, and personally inviting others to church.

Your testimony and experience with Christ are among your most powerful tools for sharing the Gospel. It's personal to you, which will make it more meaningful to others. Share what God has done in your life and let that intimate experience be a connection to telling people about Him. It's just as important to use words and to communicate who Christ is and the gift He offers to all.

Right now, you are in perhaps the greatest mission field you will ever be in. What will you do with that opportunity?

REWIND AND REJOICE

1. What are your thoughts and/or convictions about witnessing? Does it feel intimidating?

   _____
   _____
   _____

2. Who are three people you could share Jesus with this week? You could write down a specific name or a place you go to often.

   _____
   _____
   _____

3. What would be a good way to approach witnessing to someone?

   _____
   _____
   _____

AND I PRAY

Dear Lord,
I know there are so many hurting and lost people around me. Will You please give me a heart that breaks for them as Yours does? Help me see each person as You do and make space to show up for them. Please use me, God, to be a witness and share who You are. Use me, Father. Amen.

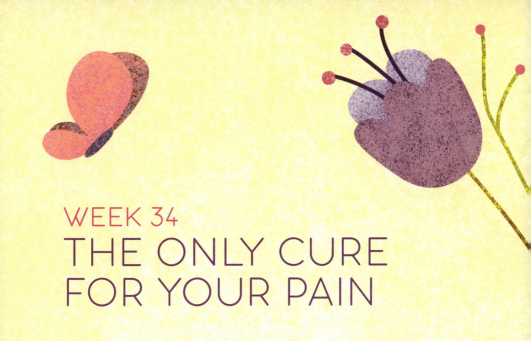

WEEK 34
THE ONLY CURE FOR YOUR PAIN

DAILY READINGS

- **Day 1: Jeremiah 29–32**
- Day 2: Jeremiah 33–36
- Day 3: Jeremiah 37–40
- Day 4: Lamentations 1–5
- Day 5: Ezekiel 1–4
- Day 6: Ezekiel 5–8
- Day 7: Catch up on any readings you've missed.

PAIN IS REAL, AND maybe you've been through something before that felt so intense you didn't think the wound would ever heal. Have you ever felt that your pain would never go away, and you'd never feel the same again?

Look what Jeremiah 30:12, 30:17 has to say about wounds:

Your wound is incurable, your injury beyond healing… But I will restore you to health and heal your wounds, declares the Lord.

How could pain and wounds be incurable in one breath and then healed the next? Let's look at the context. We see wounds cannot heal when that healing is sought in the material world. It's impossible. This basically means if you try to mask your pain with a boyfriend, alcohol or drugs, new clothes, or friends, the pain will never really heal. It might subside a little for a short time, but it will pop back up again and again.

With God, however, any wound is available for healing. Why? Because He can do anything.

Dealing with pain and brokenness face-to-face isn't easy. Few things are more challenging than recovering from a broken heart, a lost dream, or disappointment. In the darkest storms, it seems the hope of healing is the only light that has the power to pierce through like a ray of sunshine parting the storm clouds. For Christians, the hope Christ provides is our only means of survival.

The truth is that complete healing isn't possible without God. Only Christ and the Word of God can reach those broken and aching places within our souls. What path will you choose? What you choose to allow in and release back out will determine the process and completion of your healing.

Sweet girl, don't go to this world to heal your pain. Go to God, for He alone can heal you!

REWIND AND REJOICE

1. Is there something in your life that seems like it's too painful to ever heal?

2. How does this verse and devotional reframe the pain?

3. How might you press into God differently for healing?

BIBLE TRUTHS

During the thirty-three years he was on Earth, Jesus healed many people, physically and emotionally. He met the very personal needs of people such as the woman at the well (John 4) and the woman who wiped his feet with her tears and hair (Luke 7). The Gospels are filled with stories of Jesus healing the blind, the paralyzed, and even the dead. Jesus is truly a miracle worker.

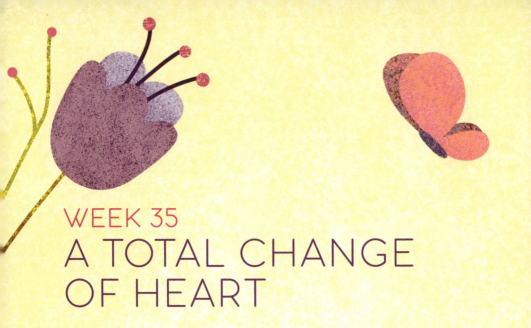

WEEK 35
A TOTAL CHANGE OF HEART

DAILY READINGS

- **Day 1: Ezekiel 9–12**
- Day 2: Ezekiel 13–16
- Day 3: Ezekiel 17–20
- Day 4: Ezekiel 21–24
- Day 5: Ezekiel 25–28
- Day 6: Ezekiel 29–32
- Day 7: Catch up on any readings you've missed.

GOD WANTS TO GIVE you a new heart. And Ezekiel shows us this powerful truth.

Ezekiel was an exile from Israel, living in a Babylonian settlement after his country was captured and his people were forced out. He was there for five years before receiving his first vision, and he would continue his prophetic ministry for twenty-two years.

There is a beautiful passage of hope in 11:16–21, a reminder that though we may be scattered, God will gather up His people and transform their hearts:

Although I sent them far away among the nations and scattered them among the countries…I will gather you from the nations and bring you back from the countries where you have been scattered, and I will give you back the land of Israel again.

The message continues:

I [God] will give them an undivided heart and put a new spirit in them; I will remove from them their heart of stone and give them a heart of flesh. Then they will follow my decrees and be careful to keep my laws. They will be my people, and I will be their God.

God will pursue you wherever you go and gather you back to Him. This means He will bring you to Himself and restore what was lost and broken. Then—and this is my favorite observation in all of Ezekiel—God will take your hard heart and give you a heart of flesh.

A "heart of stone" is said to represent a natural state of being dead to the things of God. A "heart of flesh" is said to represent a new ability to understand truth, a new desire for God, and a new spirit that loves Him. God wants to transform the old in you into new life and a new person. He wants to take our hearts—ones that have rejected, doubted, and ignored Him (maybe this is you)—and he wants to soften them so that we will desire Him. It's a complete reversal.

You can't outrun God, dear girl. You can't go so far as to never be forgiven. All it takes is turning around and taking hold of Him. And he will do incredibly wonderful work that will change your life.

REWIND AND REJOICE

1. Have you done something you regret that you hold onto or that makes you feel like God can't change your heart?

   _____
   _____
   _____
   _____

2. How does this passage reframe that understanding you've had?

   _____
   _____
   _____
   _____

3. What means the most to you from this passage in Ezekiel, and why?

   _____
   _____
   _____
   _____

LIVE IN LIGHT

1. Pray for God to turn your heart of stone into a heart of flesh.

2. Invite the Holy Spirit into your life and ask Him to help you honor God.

3. Give thanks to God this week when you notice how the Holy Spirit empowers you to do something that honors Him that you would not have been able to do on your own.

WEEK 36
COURAGE AGAINST THE CULTURE

DAILY READINGS

- Day 1: Ezekiel 33–36
- Day 2: Ezekiel 37–40
- Day 3: Ezekiel 41–44
- Day 4: Ezekiel 45–48
- **Day 5: Daniel 1–4**
- Day 6: Daniel 5–8
- Day 7: Catch up on any readings you've missed.

STANDING UP AGAINST THE culture, or peer pressure, is never easy.

The book of Daniel details the events of Daniel's life as an Israelite living in captivity in Babylon. It highlights his faithfulness to God in a faithless nation and God's care for Daniel along the way. There are some wild stories in this book!

This week's reading includes a well-known tale, one you may have heard before. King Nebuchadnezzar set up a golden image for the people to worship. When a call was made for everyone to bow to the image, Daniel's friends—Shadrach, Meshach, and Abednego—didn't. The king called them forward and threatened them with their lives. And this is how the three men responded—it's amazing!

We do not need to defend ourselves before you in this matter. If we are thrown into the blazing furnace, the God we serve is able to deliver us from it… But even if he does not, we want you to know, Your Majesty, that we will not serve your gods or worship the image of gold you have set up. ▶ **(Daniel 3:16–18)**

They trusted God in the face of death. The men were then thrown into a fire, yet they didn't burn. Instead, a Christophany (appearance of Jesus) took place. When Nebuchadnezzar saw the additional figure in the fire and all four men walking around, he called them out and declared that God was to be honored.

In another story, officials were jealous of Daniel, so they convinced King Darius to establish an edict that no one except the king could petition a man or god for thirty days. They did this because they knew Daniel prayed.

The edict went into play, and Daniel prayed. He was then captured and thrown into the lion's den. The whole night, Daniel was in the den and the king was up and fasting. At daybreak, Darius ran to the den to find Daniel alive and well! He proceeded to issue a decree that all people must fear the God of Daniel.

May you be encouraged to do the same, to stand firm in truth and grace in a culture that goes against God in every way. May you be so bold as to make a stand for Christ for others to see, not through your own wisdom or work, but rather, through the power of God. If you put your full faith and trust in God, you will not be disappointed. And who knows, maybe someone around you will turn to God along the way.

REWIND AND REJOICE

1. Have you ever had to choose between following God or giving in to peer pressure? How did you handle it?

2. How do you think Shadrach, Meshach, and Abednego felt when they were threatened with the fiery furnace? What do you learn from their response?

3. In what ways do you see our culture pressuring Christians to compromise their faith, and how do you want to respond?

VERSE FOCUS

Then King Darius wrote to all the nations...I issue a decree that in every part of my kingdom people must fear and reverence the God of Daniel. For he is the living God and he endures forever, his kingdom will not be destroyed, his dominion will never end. He rescues and he saves; he performs signs and wonders in the heavens and on the earth. He has rescued Daniel from the power of the lions. ▶ **Daniel 6:25–27**

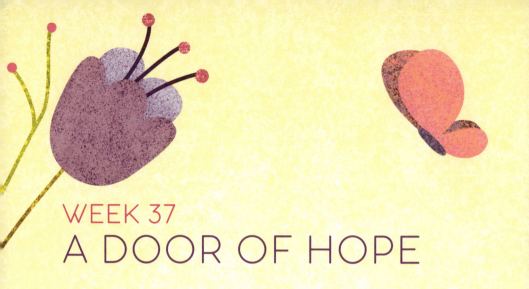

WEEK 37
A DOOR OF HOPE

DAILY READINGS

- Day 1: Daniel 9–12
- **Day 2: Hosea 1–7**
- Day 3: Hosea 8–14
- Day 4: Joel 1–3
- Day 5: Amos 1–5
- Day 6: Amos 6–9
- Day 7: Catch up on any readings you've missed.

HE WILL SHOW LOVE to us, even if we may feel unloved. This is the message of Hosea 2, a beautiful and dramatic portrayal of Israel's journey from hardship to restoration. It also powerfully parallels our own situations that may seem hopeless or fearful.

Beginning in verse 14, there is this "wooing" of Israel where God wants to bring his children close to Him and meet them on a personal level. He describes how, even in a Valley of Achor (also known as Valley of Trouble), there is a door of hope to the future. Essentially, God wants to bring you close to Him and there, in your valley of trouble and pain, show you there is this hope before you. That the trouble won't last forever.

Further, in verse 16, He discusses a transition in relationship with Him. God wants you to no longer see Him as just a master, but as a "husband." This reiterates His affection toward His people.

We then see a key phrase mentioned three times in two verses: *I will betroth you.* When a phrase or word is mentioned multiple times in a short span, it means it's very important to understand what's being said. God wants to make sure we know the importance of His covenant and restorative love.

The chapter leaves us with a confirmation that He will show love to us, even if we feel unloved.

There will be grief and pain throughout your life—and coming face to face with it won't be easy. But you can find great comfort in His words about love, redemption, and hope. Ground yourself with deep roots in this passage and allow God to draw you near to Him. Hold on to the belief that there is a door of hope just ahead and, no matter what, there is God, who deeply and passionately loves you.

God can turn your place of trouble into a door of hope. Transform your wilderness into a vineyard. Our God restores what sin destroyed and gives back what was taken. He protects you from the pests and pardons your transgressions. Such love is unmatched.

Take for yourself what Charles Spurgeon once noted of this passage: "There shall be such nearness of love, such confidence of hope, between the restored soul and her God, that she shall call him no more Baali [lord], but Ishi [husband]."

REWIND AND REJOICE

1. What do you think when you read about the valley of trouble becoming a door of hope? Does it offer you any encouragement?

   _____
   _____
   _____

2. How would you describe the difference in the relationship between a servant and their master, and a marriage?

   _____
   _____
   _____

3. What hope do you walk away with this week?

   _____
   _____
   _____

AND I PRAY

Dear Lord,
I'm so eternally grateful for Your love and Your desire to be in a relationship with me. I, too, want a meaningful relationship with You. As I draw near to You, I pray You will draw near to me and that I will find sweet security in Your presence. Amen.

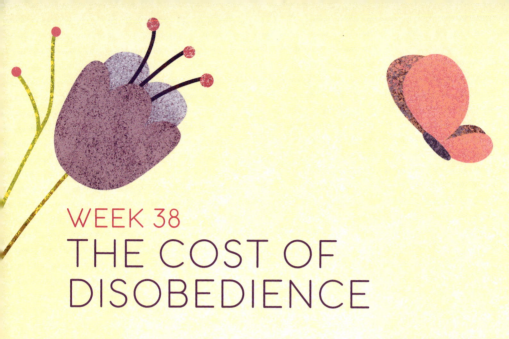

WEEK 38
THE COST OF DISOBEDIENCE

DAILY READINGS

- Day 1: Obadiah 1
- **Day 2: Jonah 1–4**
- Day 3: Micah 1–7
- Day 4: Nahum 1–3
- Day 5: Habakkuk 1–3
- Day 6: Zephaniah 1–3
- Day 7: Catch up on any readings you've missed.

WE'RE IN A LOT of different books this week, and they each have such rich text it's hard to choose one theme. But Jonah calls to us. It shows us that running from God is never the answer.

As the book goes, Jonah was called to preach God's message to the people of Nineveh. They were a group at odds with Israel, so when the call came, Jonah wasn't interested. Instead, the prophet chose to flee in the complete opposite direction of Nineveh—also known as Tarshish, in modern-day Spain. It was pretty much as far as Jonah could get from where God was asking him to go.

But he didn't get far. While on the boat, a great storm came and Jonah knew it was God, so he instructed the men to throw him overboard for their own safety. But God didn't leave him stranded in the open ocean. Instead, a great whale swallowed him up and carried him to Nineveh.

Jonah's time in the whale was one of solitude and repentance. He realized his sin and called out to God. And then he was vomited out by the whale, exactly where God wanted him all along. What's interesting is that Jonah was one of the few prophets that Jesus mentioned in the New Testament. In fact, he compared himself to Jonah, the prophet serving as a type of Christ.

While in Nineveh, Jonah preached, and an incredible thing happened: The king and the city repented. In what is considered one of the great evangelistic acts of the Bible, God saved a wicked city.

Unfortunately, Jonah wasn't entirely happy about that, as he believed they didn't deserve it. So, God taught him a lesson using a plant and a worm to show the prophet that no one was deserving, but that He was a merciful God.

We can learn from Jonah that, at times, we may want to run from God's call or directives. But God has called us to obedience. And if He must, He'll use a vehicle to carry us there, often in a challenging or painful way. May we learn to walk in obedience and mercy.

REWIND AND REJOICE

1. What are you running away from today?

   _____
   _____
   _____

2. How can you course correct from running and pivot to go in His direction?

   _____
   _____
   _____

3. What inspires you or stands out most about Jonah's time in the whale?

   _____
   _____
   _____

BIBLE TRUTHS

In Matthew 12:40–41, Jesus talks about being in the grave for the same amount of time Jonah was in the whale's belly. Just like Jonah brought God's message of repentance and salvation to the Ninevites, Jesus brought us the same message of salvation through God alone. It's a reminder that turning to God and accepting His salvation is what it's all about.

WEEK 39
CONSIDER YOUR WAYS

DAILY READINGS

- **Day 1: Haggai 1–2**
- Day 2: Zechariah 1–4
- Day 3: Zechariah 5–8
- Day 4: Zechariah 9–11
- Day 5: Zechariah 12–14
- Day 6: Malachi 1–4
- Day 7: Catch up on any readings you've missed.

CONSIDER YOUR WAYS.

This is the phrase God used twice in Haggai chapter 1, and it seems so heavy, doesn't it? Maybe it sounds like something an adult would say. But really, it's just an encouragement to consider something important—something the prophet is about to say.

When we get to Haggai, which is almost at the end of the Old Testament, the people have returned from exile; they're back in Jerusalem. They attempted to rebuild the temple, which was destroyed during their captivity, but they only got far enough to rebuild the foundation. Several outsiders opposed the project, and they gave up.

Seventeen years later, God spoke to the people through the prophet, reminding them that they needed to focus on rebuilding the temple instead of their own homes. He began by letting them know that the reason they had a hard time harvesting and building their wealth was because their priorities were misplaced. Instead, God wanted them to focus on finishing the temple. The people ended up rebuilding God's house and celebrating the Passover. It was a beautiful experience for the people, and some five hundred years later, Jesus entered that temple.

This chapter calls on you to consider your priorities. Here you are, thousands of years later, and the message still rings true for you today. Is your priority Christ? Or is it school, your hobbies, or your relationships? When God tells you to consider, it's an important message. It doesn't mean you casually think about Him or your priorities. The word "consider" means to put or set. It means setting God first and keeping Him there *on purpose*.

What we learn in Haggai is that if we attend to God and His work, He'll take care of everything else that matters.

It takes all the pressure off when you understand that seeking God first is the most important thing you can do because then everything lines up with *Him*.

REWIND AND REJOICE

1. How would you describe what happened in Haggai?

2. Is there something, or someone, who takes priority over God in your life? Share that struggle and how you might reset your focus.

3. Is there a big need you have right now that you are seeking God to help with?

LIVE IN LIGHT

1. Consider memorizing Matthew 6:33 so you can be reminded of your priorities.
2. When you find yourself becoming distracted by other things or people in a way that puts God second, remind yourself to *consider your ways*.

WEEK 40
THE REASON THIS BOOK CHANGES YOU

DAILY READINGS

- **Day 1: Matthew 1–4**
- Day 2: Matthew 5–8
- Day 3: Matthew 9–12
- Day 4: Matthew 13–16
- Day 5: Matthew 17–20
- Day 6: Matthew 21–24
- Day 7: Catch up on any readings you've missed.

JESUS. IT'S WHO THE entire Bible points to, hinges on, and proclaims in passages that don't even seem like they're talking about the Messiah. He is the very heartbeat of Scripture. And finally, you've arrived at the stories that highlight his life on earth. This is *huge* because Jesus came to earth for one reason—to save you! Even if you were the only person in the world, He would have done it again. Because you matter that much to Him.

Today, we begin not only the New Testament, but also the Gospels, which simply means "good news." That comes from the idea that Jesus brought the good news of salvation to people who were lost.

As you comb through the book of Matthew, and all the Gospels for that matter, you will get to read about the Son of God coming to earth in humble means, living a perfect life, and becoming a substitute for our sins on the cross.

And that's what I want to focus on today—the atonement for our sins. Don't get me wrong, reading about His birth fosters a bit of warmth. His life was powerful and full of the miraculous. But none of that would have mattered if He hadn't died on the cross and risen again.

"Substitutionary atonement" is a big phrase, and it means something even bigger. Jesus became the perfect sacrificial lamb who atoned for your sin by becoming a substitute. Because of that sacrifice, you don't have to suffer an eternity away from God. He took your place, took all your sins, died, and conquered death to gain the victory needed for you to be made right with God. It is available to everyone if they will simply turn to Jesus and follow Him in obedience.

What Jesus did changed everything about your life. It's your eternal destination, certainly, but it also affects how you should live, the choices you make, and even the places you go. It's the very thing that should live in your mind every single day. What motivates you and guides your life in such a way that it honors Him?

Are you living like His death means everything to you? I want to encourage you to live with eternity in mind, thinking about how your choices and actions shape a life well lived. It's called a "living sacrifice." Reflecting on Jesus often will radically change your life.

REWIND AND REJOICE

1. How would you describe substitutionary atonement in your own words, and the sacrifice Jesus made on your behalf?

2. What do you think about that? Does it move something inside of you?

3. Write out a prayer of thanksgiving for the sacrifice Jesus made on the cross and His love, which changes everything for you.

VERSE FOCUS

He is not here; he has risen, just as he said. ▶ **Matthew 28:6**

WEEK 41
THE GREAT COMMANDMENT

DAILY READINGS

- Day 1: Matthew 25–28
- Day 2: Mark 1–4
- Day 3: Mark 5–8
- **Day 4: Mark 9–12**
- Day 5: Mark 13–16
- Day 6: Luke 1–4
- Day 7: Catch up on any readings you've missed.

HAVE YOU EVER HEARD of The Great Commandment? It's important in Scripture, but it's also referenced in the secular world, so it's sort of a big deal. What's cool is that it boils everything down into a short mission statement, because sometimes it can feel overwhelming to remember and do everything in the Bible. I get it. Yes, the entire Bible is important and should be obeyed, but sometimes, if you simply think about doing what The Great Commandment says, it can help you live out so much of what is in the Bible in a lot of ways (Matthew 22:40). It's definitely worth knowing.

Here it is—Mark 12:28-31:

"Of all the commandments, which is the most important?"... "'Love the Lord your God with all your heart and with all your soul and with all your mind and with all your strength.' The second is this: 'Love your neighbor as yourself.' There is no commandment greater than these."

Let's break down the two commands here:

1. Love God first and foremost with everything you are and have.
2. Love everyone.

First, you are called to love Him more than anyone or anything else. It should be everything your life hinges on, don't you think? And then, from there, you love your neighbor. But "neighbor" is really just another word for everyone, and you must love them as you love yourself.

Think about how much you think about yourself. How you're always looking to benefit yourself and make sure you're taken care of. Now apply that to everyone else. How can you love people to the extent that it matches how you love yourself?

What we see, too, is that you can't really love people to the fullest without Jesus. You love him, God's power flows through you, and in that power is the ability to love people beyond human capability.

The book of Mark references loving others in the importance of serving them. Mark 10:43–45 tells us serving others was Jesus's greatest mission:

Whoever wants to become great among you must be your servant, and whoever wants to be first must be slave of all. For even the Son of Man did not come to be served, but to serve, and to give his life as a ransom for many.

Your life isn't meant to be only about you. It's meant to be lived for God and for others. Consider how that might change how you live your day-to-day life: how you show your faith at school, how you stand up for others in the lunchroom, and how you respond to disagreements with your parents or teachers. This commandment is meant to shape everything you do and say, so will you let it?

REWIND AND REJOICE

1. What does it look like to love God with all your heart, mind, soul, and strength?

2. What does it look like to love someone like you love yourself?

3. How does this understanding change how you live your day-to-day life?

AND I PRAY

Dear Lord,
You have given me such great tools for living the kind of life You desire. Would you please help me use those tools wisely? I want to keep You first in my life and find a capacity to love others that I haven't known before. Please help me, God, give all of my life to You and serve others in such a way that they look to You. Amen.

WEEK 42
THE WORLD DOESN'T HAVE IT

DAILY READINGS

- **Day 1: Luke 5–8**
- Day 2: Luke 9–11
- Day 3: Luke 12–14
- **Day 4: Luke 15–18**
- Day 5: Luke 19–21
- Day 6: Luke 22–24
- Day 7: Catch up on any readings you've missed.

HAVE YOU EVER PACKED for a trip and realized you brought way too much stuff? Like, you have five pairs of shoes for a two-day trip, three different jackets "just in case," and enough snacks to feed a small army? We all tend to overpack because we think we might need everything we own, right?

But here's the thing: When it comes to our faith journey, we don't need all that extra stuff. In fact, Jesus tells us that the world and all its things can't really provide what we need, and we shouldn't try to take it with us. Let's take a look at what the Gospel of Luke has to say about this.

First, in Luke 8, there is a woman who had been bleeding for twelve years nonstop. Sounds pretty horrible, doesn't it? This issue with blood affected her whole life: what she did, where she could go, and who she could be with. Because, at this time in history, a person who bled was seen as unclean. Which meant she wouldn't have been able to go to the temple or touch anyone without making them unclean. Terrible, right?

In verse 43, we read that the woman *spent all she had on doctors and yet could not be healed by any* (CSB). She literally spent everything she had, tried everything the world could offer to cure her, but nothing worked. Then, with one touch of Jesus, she was instantly healed. It's so beautiful! Only God could truly help her.

Then you have the rich young ruler in Luke 18. He asked Jesus how he could inherit eternal life. Jesus responded in verse 22: *Sell everything you have and give to the poor, and you will have treasure in heaven. Then come, follow me.*

If you read just before this, the man was already moral, but it wasn't enough. Jesus asked him to give everything he had to follow Christ, but the man wasn't willing. It was less about the money and more about the condition of the heart. He wasn't willing to let the world go to follow Jesus. He wasn't about The Great Commandment.

So, what does this look like for you, a girl living thousands of years later? I would say two things.

1. The world doesn't hold the answer to your problems (although, for clarification, God can use practical means to help, such as doctors when you're sick or an anonymous donation for your mission trip).

2. The world can't save you, so why hold onto it?

I get it: The world is enticing, and for that reason, almost everyone lives for it. But it's unable to solve our current problems *and* our eternal problems. And anyway, it's unable to truly fulfill us. Remember what Solomon said? It's all meaningless.

REWIND AND REJOICE

1. Have you been looking for an answer in the world that you now realize can only be found in God?

   _____
   _____
   _____

2. What are you trying to hold onto in this world?

   _____
   _____
   _____

3. What inspires you most about these two stories in Luke?

   _____
   _____
   _____

BIBLE TRUTHS

In a few verses from the rich young ruler, Jesus tells the disciples in Luke 18:29–30 that anyone who gives up the world and the things or people in it will receive many times more than what they lost. That's a promise you can hold onto, that your sacrifice will be rewarded.

WEEK 43
REJECTED FOR YOUR FAITH

DAILY READINGS

- Day 1: John 1–4
- Day 2: John 5–8
- Day 3: John 9–12
- **Day 4: John 13–17**
- Day 5: John 18–21
- Day 6: Acts 1–3
- Day 7: Catch up on any readings you've missed.

If they persecuted me, they will persecute you also. ▶ **John 15:20**

HAVE YOU EVER FELT pressured, persecuted, or judged because of your faith? Maybe you pulled back from gossiping in the locker room, and the other girls called you out for being too nice. Or you wanted to pray before a game but were told you were not allowed. Perhaps you've literally been made fun of for loving Jesus. These are all real possibilities and more common than you might think.

You and I live in a world that thrives on resisting God. Satan greatly influences people, our culture, and ideas. He literally seeks to resist God and destroy people—that is his goal. Which means life isn't going to be easy for a Christian.

Jesus makes this point in an amazing speech during the Last Supper (John 15). He tells the disciples that the world will hate them because the world hates Him. If they looked like the world, the world wouldn't mind it; in fact, they would celebrate it. But because people choose to look like Christ rather than the world, they are rejected.

This means that there will be times in your life when you are rejected, persecuted, and judged because you call yourself a Christian. Situations will offend you. People will overlook you. It will hurt and it might cost you something. But they do it, not because of you, but because they have rejected Christ.

At times, you may feel like questioning your faith or giving in to peer pressure, but you must remain steadfast. Fight the good fight, finish the race, keep your faith, and you will receive your reward (2 Timothy 4:7–8).

If you ask me, I'd rather be associated with Christ than anyone else.

REWIND AND REJOICE

1. Have you ever felt judged for your faith or felt opposition because you follow Jesus? Describe what that was like.

2. What situations could arise in your life right now that feel like persecution, and how will you handle those moments?

3. What encouragement do these readings offer for moments of persecution?

LIVE IN LIGHT

1. Be a light and a witness to the people you meet this week.
2. In moments you sense resistance to your faith, hold on to the hope you have in Jesus.
3. Spend time this week focusing on praying for those who are persecuted around the world for their faith.

WEEK 44
LEARNING FROM OTHERS

DAILY READINGS

- Day 1: Acts 4–7
- Day 2: Acts 8–10
- Day 3: Acts 11–13
- **Day 4: Acts 14–16**
- Day 5: Acts 17–19
- Day 6: Acts 20–22
- Day 7: Catch up on any readings you've missed.

LET'S TALK ABOUT SOMETHING that's not always the easiest to hear: Instruction. Yeah, it can be a bit of a downer sometimes, but it's also a super important way for God to shape and grow us, even if it doesn't feel great in the moment. But trust me, it's totally worth it in the end.

Learning to lean into instruction is one of the best things you can do as a Christian.

This week we're in the book of Acts, which is an account of the early Church. Jesus had gone to heaven, and the Gospel was spreading like wildfire. People were getting saved and baptized in the Holy Spirit all over the place; it was amazing.

There's Apollos, who was going around and telling people about God, and he really nailed this principle of receiving instruction, as told in Acts 18:24-28.

Apollos was all in for God. He knew his stuff about the Old Testament and was a follower of John the Baptist. He was passionate about sharing God's word and was on fire for his mission. But when Priscilla and Aquila heard him teach, they realized he was missing some key points about Christian beliefs. Instead of letting him continue with incomplete knowledge, they pulled him aside and filled him in on the full story of Jesus.

Apollos could've been, "Hey, I've got this!" But he wasn't. He listened, took their advice to heart, and let it shape his teachings moving forward. Because of that, he became an even stronger voice for God.

How do you handle instruction? Do you push back or do you take it in and think about it? Do you let it help you grow? I hope you do. Being open to correction can make a huge difference in your life and how far you can go with God's plan for you. We see in Scripture that when you embrace instruction, you become a more powerful witness; your influence increases.

Yeah, getting feedback isn't always a blast, but how you react to it can really set the path for your future. Having a teachable spirit will help you go further and do more amazing things. So, embrace instruction and keep growing, because it will lead to favor and opportunity to impact the kingdom you can't even imagine.

REWIND AND REJOICE

1. Read the story of Apollos and come back here to write what you observe.

   _____
   _____
   _____

2. How do you think his story would be different if he had not received instruction?

   _____
   _____
   _____

3. Do you find yourself rejecting instruction from a particular person or in a particular area of your life? Where and how can you shift your approach?

   _____
   _____
   _____

VERSE FOCUS

Whoever gives heed to instruction prospers, and blessed is the one who trusts in the Lord. ▶ **Proverbs 16:20**

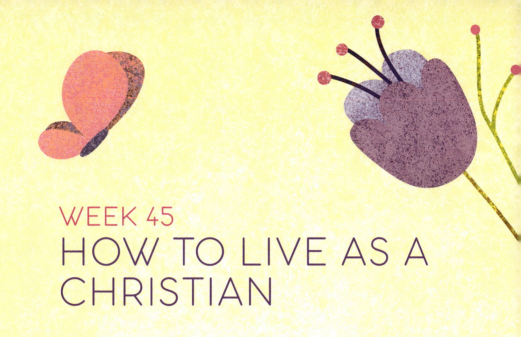

WEEK 45
HOW TO LIVE AS A CHRISTIAN

DAILY READINGS

- [ ] Day 1: Acts 23–25
- [ ] Day 2: Acts 26–28
- [ ] Day 3: Romans 1–3
- [ ] Day 4: Romans 4–7
- [ ] Day 5: Romans 8–10
- [x] **Day 6: Romans 11–13**
- [ ] Day 7: Catch up on any readings you've missed.

PICTURE THIS: You've got a bunch of ingredients in your kitchen, and you want to make a delicious meal. Each ingredient is important, but it's how you mix them together that really makes the magic happen.

In Romans 12:9–21, Paul gives us a recipe for living a life full of love and good deeds; it's noted as "Christian ethics." Basically, it's like handing us a list of ingredients and instructions for how to live out our faith in a way that really works.

Paul started with, *Love must be sincere. Hate what is evil; cling to what is good* (Romans 12:9). It's pretty straightforward. He's saying to make sure your love is genuine and to focus on what's truly good. One way to do this is to *Honor one another above yourselves* (Romans 12:10). This means to start with loving others. Remind you of The Greatest Commandment, perhaps?

Then he added some more tips: Be joyful in hope, be patient, help others, and live peacefully with everyone. It's all about blending these qualities together to create a life that reflects God's love.

But let's break it down a bit and focus on:
- Joy
- Patience and perseverance
- Loving others and living in harmony with them
- Doing what is good

This is the life God has called you to live. And the thing is, the world will fight this kind of living. But you get to choose. As you walk through your school's hallways, interact with people on your team or at work, and even in your own home, choose to practice these ethics as you've been instructed.

As you go forth this week, think about how you can use these "ingredients" to make your life meaningful.

REWIND AND REJOICE

1. What stood out to you most in this passage of Scripture and the devotional?

2. Is there one ethic you struggle with more than the others, and how could you grow in that area?

3. Do you think the world will go easy on you when you try to live this kind of life?

AND I PRAY

Dear Lord,
I'm so grateful that You equip me to live the life You desire. I truly want to honor what You've given and live a life that honors You. Please help me to be attentive to this passage of Scripture and weave these principles into my life. Thank you, Holy Spirit, for Your continued work in my life. Amen.

WEEK 46
WARNING AGAINST SIN AND TEMPTATION

DAILY READINGS

- Day 1: Romans 14–16
- Day 2: 1 Corinthians 1–4
- **Day 3: 1 Corinthians 5–8**
- Day 4: 1 Corinthians 9–12
- Day 5: 1 Corinthians 13–16
- Day 6: 2 Corinthians 1–4
- Day 7: Catch up on any readings you've missed.

"I have the right to do anything," you say—but not everything is beneficial. "I have the right to do anything"—but I will not be mastered by anything. ▶ **1 Corinthians 6:12**

THIS WEEK, WE'RE GOING TO TALK about something that might hit close to home: making choices. Think about a time when you had to make a choice—maybe it was deciding which class to take, how to spend your free time, or even what to wear for a special occasion. Sometimes it's hard to know which choice is best, right?

In 1 Corinthians 6:12, Paul reminds us that while we have the freedom to make choices, not every choice is going to be the most helpful or positive for us. And not everything is worth doing.

Paul shared these thoughts after discussing sinful living. He mentioned that the unrighteous engage in sexual immorality, theft, greed, drunkenness, abuse, and deception. These people would not inherit the kingdom of God. They had the choice to live how they wanted—it was called "free will"—but they chose to live their lives unwisely, and that had a great cost.

The good news is that those who choose to follow Christ are washed, sanctified, and justified in Christ. Meaning you have been cleansed from your sins, made holy, and made right by Jesus. And because of that very gift, you should now go forth being choosy about how you live.

Technically, you can do things that are unrighteous. But because you are made right, you should now choose to live differently. When you're tempted to sin, you choose to go the other way. Your choices are now filtered through God's Word. And you have that freedom because you are not mastered by sin but made free in Christ.

I simply want to encourage you to make the best choices out there. It's tough, I know. I've had my own share of failures, and I regret them all. But God has been faithful to a repentant heart, and I want to encourage you to make the better choice—which you can by the Spirit of God that lives in you.

REWIND AND REJOICE

1. What are your thoughts about 1 Corinthians 6:12?

   _____
   _____
   _____

2. What would be some upcoming choices that you should filter through this passage?

   _____
   _____
   _____

3. How will this verse influence your life moving forward?

   _____
   _____
   _____

BIBLE TRUTHS

The end of chapter 6 says, in verses 19-20, *Do you not know that your bodies are temples of the Holy Spirit, who is in you, whom you have received from God? You are not your own; you were bought at a price. Therefore honor God with your bodies.* As a believer, the Holy Spirit lives in you, so your body is a temple. Isn't that wild and also insanely beautiful?! Honor that temple and honor Him with your choices.

WEEK 47
THE COMPARISON TRAP

DAILY READINGS

- Day 1: 2 Corinthians 5–9
- Day 2: 2 Corinthians 10–13
- Day 3: Galatians 1–3
- **Day 4: Galatians 4–6**
- Day 5: Ephesians 1–6
- Day 6: Philippians 1–4
- Day 7: Catch up on any readings you've missed.

YOU ARE UNIQUE, AND I mean that sincerely. When God formed you in your mother's womb, He did so with great care and detail. He knew the gifts being woven into you and the experiences that would shape you, including the hard ones. God knew what part you would play in the body of Christ, and it was unique to *you*.

Sometimes, we get caught up in what other people are doing or being used for. We wish we had their talents or opportunities. We wish we had made the team instead of them. We wish those girls had chosen us to be in their friend group.

Comparison is a trap. One thing it does really well is get us to question our identity and purpose. But the lane others run in wasn't meant for you, and yours wasn't meant for them. Never try to be a copycat—be you.

I absolutely love the way *The Message* translates Galatians 6:4–5.

Make a careful exploration of who you are and the work you have been given, and then sink yourself into that. Don't be impressed with yourself. Don't compare yourself with others. Each of you must take responsibility for doing the creative best you can with your own life.

Scripture encourages us to take a moment and really think about who God has made us to be. It's not about comparing ourselves to others but, instead, discovering our own unique gifts and talents. What are the things you're good at? What's your special story and experience? God has given you a unique set of skills and a personal journey that He wants to use in a special way.

Once you figure out what makes you tick and what you're passionate about, focus on that. Don't worry about what your friends are doing. Dive into what God has planned for you and give it your all. Stay confident in God's amazing plan for you. Trust that everything will fall into place exactly as it should because God is behind it all. That way, we can celebrate His power and not just our own efforts.

Lean into Galatians 6 today, trust in the dreams God has placed in your heart, and embrace the journey right in front of you.

REWIND AND REJOICE

1. In what areas do you find yourself comparing to others or downplaying your gifts?

2. How does this passage and devotion shift how you feel?

3. What gift can you start offering to the Body of Christ?

LIVE IN LIGHT

1. When you notice that you are comparing yourself to other people this week, remind yourself to take responsibility for what has been given to you.

2. When comparison creeps in, flip the script and celebrate the other person.

WEEK 48
BATTLING YOUR THOUGHTS

DAILY READINGS

- **Day 1: Colossians 1–4**
- Day 2: 1 Thessalonians 1–3
- Day 3: 1 Thessalonians 4–5
- Day 4: 2 Thessalonians 1–3
- Day 5: 1 Timothy 1–3
- Day 6: 1 Timothy 4–6
- Day 7: Catch up on any readings you've missed.

HAVE YOU EVER WONDERED how to combat the negative thoughts that enter your mind? I've got just the verse to help! It's Colossians 3:2: *Set your minds on things above, not on earthly things.*

I know, I know, it sounds so simple. But does it really work? I can confirm that, yes, it does. Here's how.

When you have a negative thought—judging a girl at school, an urge to disrespect your parent, an inkling of temptation, thinking highly of yourself—you want to take that thought captive, as 2 Corinthians 10 encourages. This means you take that thought to God because God can overcome it. And you can do that in a couple of ways:

1. Pray, and ask God to help you.

2. Switch out that thought for something eternal-minded or a verse to combat the idea.

That's it. It sounds so simple, but it really does help so much. The next time you start judging a girl at school, pray for her. When you feel the urge to disrespect your parents, remember what Scripture says about honoring them. When temptation knocks at the door, remember all things are possible but not beneficial. When you think highly of yourself, invite God to help you fight pride.

Learning to take your negative thoughts captive and switch them out will be a game changer for you and your mind. You'll notice less comparison, fewer rogue thoughts, and less pride, while also finding more peace, more goodness, and more ponderings of God.

REWIND AND REJOICE

1. What recurring thought should you take captive?

2. How can you do that—what's a practical way to take that thought captive?

3. Write down a verse you would like to memorize that you can quote in moments when your thoughts need to switch.

VERSE FOCUS

We demolish arguments and every pretension that sets itself up against the knowledge of God, and we take captive every thought to make it obedient to Christ. ▶ **2 Corinthians 10:5**

WEEK 49
OVERCOMING FEAR

DAILY READINGS

- **Day 1: 2 Timothy 1–4**
- Day 2: Titus 1–3
- Day 3: Philemon 1
- Day 4: Hebrews 1–3
- Day 5: Hebrews 4–6
- Day 6: Hebrews 7–9
- Day 7: Catch up on any readings you've missed.

I REMEMBER ONCE, WHEN I was nineteen years old, I was going in for a job interview for a summer gig. And I was sitting in my car, so afraid of this interview with a big company and trying to give myself a pep talk. Want to know what I used to help me through that moment? A verse from 2 Timothy 1:7: *For God has not given us a spirit of fear, but one of power, love, and sound judgment* (CSB).

This verse is a powerful reminder that fear can be overcome. Now, I don't know if you've ever been afraid of a job interview like I was, but maybe you've been afraid at school tryouts, of a bully at school, or perhaps of a math test. Fear doesn't just exist in the dark or when there is trouble, although that happens too. It can pop up in your daily life when you feel anxious or nervous.

This verse doesn't say it's wrong to be afraid, but it does say that God didn't create you to live in fear. You can feel emotions because they usually point you to something real in your life, but that's where they end. That's when you decide to take that feeling to God and run the situation through His Word and what He says.

In fear, remind yourself that God didn't make you a fearful person and that you can choose to live your life through the power of the Holy Spirit.

Here's what you can do the next time you're afraid:

1. Go to God and ask Him to help you. Perhaps even remind yourself of this verse as a tool to fight the fear.

2. God has given you the ability to think about things with sensibility and a clear mind instead of anxiety or fear. So, hold that situation up against God and remind yourself of all the things you've learned in Scripture about God, and see that your fear is not as big as Him.

Fear doesn't have to be in the driver's seat of your life, and it shouldn't be. Invite the Holy Spirit to lead the way, and you'll be in good hands.

REWIND AND REJOICE

1. Is there a situation right now that causes a bit of fear in your life?

   _____
   _____
   _____

2. How can you work through that from what you've learned?

   _____
   _____
   _____

3. What encourages you most from this verse in 2 Timothy 1?

   _____
   _____
   _____

AND I PRAY

Dear Lord,
Thank You for giving me a spirit of power, love, and sound mind. Please help me overcome fear in my life. I want to live my life trusting you and not letting fear lead. Greater are You than anything in this world, and I know I am in good hands. Amen.

WEEK 50
HEARING AND DOING

DAILY READINGS

- Day 1: Hebrews 10–11
- Day 2: Hebrews 12–13
- **Day 3: James 1–3**
- Day 4: James 4–5
- Day 5: 1 Peter 1–5
- Day 6: 2 Peter 1–3
- Day 7: Catch up on any readings you've missed.

HAVE YOU EVER HAD your parents or a teacher ask you to do something, and you acknowledge what they say, but then you forget and don't do it? Doesn't usually work out for you, does it? Well, we see in James that we can do the same with God.

You've been in the Bible for almost a full year now, and that's amazing! Truly, what you're doing to invest in God's Word is one of the most important things you could do with your life. But also, what good is it if you're not putting into practice what God is teaching you?

James says in chapter 1, hey, first and foremost, be doers of the Word. And it's more than just actions; James emphasizes that being doers should characterize a person's entire personality.

As a believer, people should be able to look at your life and know that you are someone living in the Word, who does what the Word says, and who walks in that consistent righteousness we are called to.

James says we should be doers because those who just hear have deceived themselves. The word "deceived" means there was a miscalculation. Christians who only hear, but don't do, have made a serious miscalculation about what it means to truly be a believer.

Then James gives this analogy: *Anyone who listens to the word but does not do what it says is like someone who looks at his face in a mirror and, after looking at himself, goes away and immediately forgets what he looks like* (James 1:23-24).

What does this mean exactly? Well, there are people who look at God's Word but walk away immediately and not only forget what it said but also don't *do* what it said. So, you can be intentionally looking to learn but still walk away unaffected. The person who only hears God's word without doing it has the same sense as a person who looks into a mirror and immediately forgets what they saw. The information didn't do any good in their life.

The doer, in contrast, looks intently at the Word as perfect and full, and does what God has outlined in Scripture. A healthy

Christian looks into God's Word to do something about it, not just store facts.

How do we summarize this?

1. HEAR: To hear God's Word, you must be *in* God's Word, which you are. You're halfway there.

2. DO: If God tells you to be kind, do it. Give, go to church, serve, worship, do it. *Be a doer*.

That's what obedience looks like. It's saying, I'm going to do this even though I don't want to, or even though it's not popular, or even though it's hard. I'm doing it because my God has said to. And that's more important than anything else.

REWIND AND REJOICE

1. Do you find yourself struggling at times to put into practice what you're learning in the Bible?

   _____
   _____
   _____

2. What is one thing you can take with you this week to *do*?

   _____
   _____
   _____

3. Verse 25 says that the person who does will be blessed. How do you think that looks in real life?

_____

_____

_____

BIBLE TRUTHS

James was Jesus's half brother. Did you know that he didn't believe Jesus was the Messiah for a long time? It wasn't until he saw Jesus resurrected that he believed. From there, he became a great leader in the early church.

WEEK 51
EFFECTIVE PRAYER

DAILY READINGS

- **Day 1: 1 John 1–5**
- Day 2: 2 John 1
- Day 3: 3 John 1
- Day 4: Jude 1
- Day 5: Revelation 1–3
- Day 6: Revelation 4–6
- Day 7: Catch up on any readings you've missed.

JOHN IS ABOUT TO take us into Revelation with text rich in prophecy and drenched in judgment. But just before we get there, we get these letters he wrote—1, 2, and 3 John—where he talks a lot about love. He has this beautiful discourse in 1 John 4 about knowing God through love. This is a passage you might want to sit with this week (and beyond) because it's like a love letter for *you*. A love letter about how God literally *is* love and how he gave an example of that love by sending Jesus.

Sandwiched in between this love letter and Revelation is a quick mention of effective prayer in 1 John 5:14–15. Before we end this incredible journey together, how could I not talk about prayer in detail? You're going to need it.

So, what does John say? He starts by saying in verse 14, *This is the confidence we have before him.* Here's what that means for you: When you go to God in prayer, you can be confident. And you can be confident because when you pray in accordance with His will, He hears you. Quite the beautiful promise, isn't it?

But did you catch the disclaimer *according to his will*? Let's sit with this for a minute. You can pray for anything, but that doesn't mean God will respond how you want Him to. But that's one of the incredible things about reading the Bible and praying regularly: You begin to bend your will to His. You begin to want what He wants and pray for things to work out how He wants them to.

My friend Jennifer Edewaard has this quote, and I say it to myself all the time: *His plan. His path. His pace.*

When you begin to adopt this mindset, you begin to pray His will—and not just His will, either, but His way and in His timing. And when you're praying His will, of course, He is going to act to answer that prayer.

I want to encourage you today to start praying for His will. Yes, you have needs and desires, and certainly, pray about those things. But pray for God to help you pray for those things in a way that He wants to work it out. That it's not about you getting what you want, but about God providing what He sees is best.

Praying for His will means you can have confidence that God will respond. What better provision and hope is there than that for the rest of your life?

REWIND AND REJOICE

1. How does this passage influence your prayer life and understanding of prayer?

2. Does it change how you are praying for something in your life right now?

3. Note the connection with love in 1 John 4 and prayer in 1 John 5.

LIVE IN LIGHT

Make a list of three major prayer requests for the week, and as you pray for them, ask God to shape your heart to pray for them however He longs to work in those situations.

WEEK 52
LIVING WITH ETERNITY IN MIND

DAILY READINGS

- Day 1: Revelation 7–9
- Day 2: Revelation 10–12
- Day 3: Revelation 13–15
- Day 4: Revelation 16–18
- Day 5: Revelation 19–20
- **Day 6: Revelation 21–22**
- Day 7: Catch up on any readings you've missed.

VACATIONS ARE PRETTY GREAT, RIGHT? The escape from your normal and the discovery of new places is fun.

Now, I don't know about you, but sometimes I find the anticipation for the trip just as exciting as the trip itself, if not more so. Have you ever had that happen? Sometimes, dreaming up the excitement is actually more fun than doing it.

But one thing will turn out way better than we can imagine: HEAVEN.

Revelation is one big vision that God presents to John the disciple. It's packed with prophecy of what's to come, both judgment and hope. The current world and its fall will be replaced with a new, perfect earth. And there's this hope for those who profess Christ as Lord and Savior that one day they will spend eternity with God in heaven.

Revelation 21 talks about a new heaven and a new earth God is creating right now. It will be paradise. There will be no pain, no suffering—only harmony and joy. God will live with His people. Sin will be out of the picture. Sounds amazing, right?

As you wrap up your year in the Bible, I want to encourage you to remember this is only the beginning. You have an eternity with God coming, and it will be perfect, free, and better than anything you can imagine.

Go from this journey excited about where you're ultimately going. Live with eternity in mind. Doing so will shape your choices and how you live your life. It will also help you stay faithful in the face of opposition because you know that anything on earth is only temporary.

There's something truly powerful about living with the end in mind. But the end is just the beginning. Heaven will be your dwelling place with God, and that's something to be excited about!

I hope your journey in Scripture has been meaningful to you and has made a big impact in your life, your relationship with God, and your walk. Stay the course, sweet girl. Remember that God is trustworthy and faithful, and He desires to walk with you. Make that relationship the most important thing in the world to you and you won't regret it.

REWIND AND REJOICE

1. What makes you excited about eternity?

___

2. How does living with an eternal mindset influence how you live?

___

3. How has this devotional impacted your life the most?

VERSE FOCUS

"'He will wipe every tear from their eyes. There will be no more death' or mourning or crying or pain, for the old order of things has passed away." ▸ Revelation 21:4

GROUP STUDY GUIDE

1. What part of the Bible have you read recently that really spoke to you?
2. Can you share a Bible story that has impacted you and why?
3. How do you think God is trying to speak to you through the Bible right now?
4. What one verse has been on your mind lately? Why do you think that is?
5. How do you apply what you read in the Bible to your daily life?
6. Have you ever felt that a Bible passage was written just for you? What was it?
7. What is a new thing you've learned about God or your faith from the Bible this week?
8. Can you recall a time when reading the Bible brought you comfort or guidance?
9. Is there a Bible character you relate to? What makes you feel connected to them?
10. How does reading the Bible help you understand God's plan for your life?
11. What is one way you can share what you've learned from the Bible with others?

12. How has your understanding of a particular Bible story changed over time?
13. What does your current Bible reading say about God's character?
14. How do you feel God is challenging you through the Bible?
15. What Bible verse gives you strength in difficult times?
16. How do you think God wants you to grow through your Bible study?
17. How do you see the Bible influencing the decisions you make?
18. What does the Bible teach you about loving others?
19. How does the Bible help you deal with stress or anxiety?
20. What's a misconception about the Bible that you've encountered and how do you address it?

RESOURCES

BOOKS

- *A Girl's Life with God* by Casey Gibbons
- *The Power of a Praying Girl* by Stormie Omartian

WEBSITES

Brio Magazine: A teen girl's magazine from Focus on the Family. *store.focusonthefamily.com/brio-magazine*

Lifeway Girls Ministry: An online catalog of Bible studies and resources for teen girls. *lifeway.com/en/shop/ministries/girls*

Theos Youth: Biblically sound theology videos and courses for youth. My number one recommended resource! *theosu.ca*

TBNx: A Christian digital network for teens, including the show Girl Talk. *instagram.com/tbnxofficial*

INDEX

A
Abednego, 127
Abraham, 3, 7–9, 11
Abram, 3
Acts, 155
   18:24–28, 155
anointing, 113
anxiety, 110–111. *See also* fear
Apollos, 155
Aquila, 155
atonement, 3, 23, 141–142

B
Babylon, 123, 127
Bible
   books in, xi
   daily readings, xii, xiii–xiv
   marking up, xii, xiii
   translations of, xi, xiii
blessings, 113–114
Boaz, 40, 45

C
Caleb, 27
cedar trees, 92–93
choices, 161–162
Christian ethics, 158–159
Christophany, 127

1 Chronicles
   11, 62
2 Chronicles
   20:15, 17, 66
Colossians
   3:2, 167
comparison trap, 164–165
converts, 38
1 Corinthians
   6:12, 161
   6:19–20, 162
2 Corinthians
   10:5, 168
courage, 34–36, 127–129
Creation, 3
cultural pressures, 127–129

D
Daniel, 127
   3:16–18, 127
   6:25–27, 129
Darius, 127
dating, 106–108
David, 40, 52–53, 62, 95
Deuteronomy
   31:6, 34
disobedience, 27, 135–136
doers, 173–175
doubt, 15–17

E

Ecclesiastes, 98
    2:10–11, 108
Edewaard, Jennifer, 177
Egypt, 11, 15, 19
Elijah, 55
encouragement, 45–47, 82–83
English Standard Version (ESV), xiii
Ephesians
    3:20–21, 47
Esther, 72
    4:14, 72
    4:16, 73
eternity, 180–182
evil, 92
Exodus, 15
    6:6–7, 17
Ezekiel, 123
    11:16–21, 123
Ezra, 69

F

faith, 38–39, 152–153
faithfulness, 49–50, 82–83
Fall, 3
fear
    letting go of, 34–36
    overcoming, 170–171
feedback, 155–156
feelings and emotions, 86–87, 170
feeling seen, 11–13
Flood, 3
forgiveness, 52, 124
forgotten, feeling of being, 11–13
free will, 161
friendships, 62–64

G

Galatians
    6:4–5, 164
Genesis, 3
    15:6, 3
gifts, 42–43
giving thanks, 110–111
God
    hearing the Word of, 173–175
    His plan for you, 15–17, 42–43
    love for, 144–146
    love of, 131–133
    mercy of, 3, 9
    refuge in, 31–32
    rejecting, 59–60
    relationship with, 3, 42–43, 95–96, 131–133
    righteousness of, 23
    standing firm in, 66–67
    trust in, 3–5, 7–9, 13, 49, 66–67, 110–111
    will of, 177–178
golden calf, 19
good news, 141
Gospels, 141, 148
grace, 23
gratitude, 29
Great Commandment, 144–146, 158
group study, xiv, 185–186

H

Hagar, 9
Haggai, 138
hard times, 89–90
healing, 120–121
heart of stone/heart of flesh, 123–125
Heaven, 180

Hebrews
  11:19, 7
  11:31, 38
holiness, 23–24
Holy Spirit, 170
hope, 131–133
Hosea
  2:14, 131
  2:16, 131
House of Bread, 45
humility, 69–70

I

idols, 19–21
instruction, 155–156
Isaac, 3, 7–9
Isaiah
  26:3, 110
  55:11, x
  61:1, 113
Ishmael, 9
Israel, 23, 27, 42, 52, 59, 82, 123
Israelites, 19, 34, 38, 69, 72, 127

J

James, 173, 175
  1:23–24, 173
  4:5, 69
Jehoshaphat, 66, 67
Jeremiah
  20:9, 117
  30:12, 17, 120
Jericho, 38
Jerusalem, 59, 69
Jesus
  ancestry of, 40
  Christophany, 127
  healing by, 121
  as the perfect sacrifice, 25
  substitutionary atonement of, 141–142
Job, 75–77, 79–80
  1:21, 75
  1:22, 75
  38:4–7, 79
John
  3:16–17, 32
  4, 121
  15, 93, 152
  15:20, 152
1 John
  2:20, 113
  5:14–15, 177
John the Baptist, 155
Jonah, 135
Jonathan, 62
Jordan River, 38
Joseph, 3, 11–12, 40, 49
Joshua, 27, 34, 38, 42
Judah, 40, 59, 66, 67
Judges, 42
  21:25, 42
judgment, 152–153

K

1 Kings
  8, 52
  18–19, 55
2 Kings
  17:7, 59

L

Levites, 23
Leviticus, 23, 25
  20:26, 23
living sacrifice, 142

love
  of God, 131–133
  for God, 144–146
  of neighbor, 144–146
  romantic, 106–108
low points, 55–57
Luke
  4:14–20, 115
  7, 121
  8:43, 148
  18:22, 148
  18:29–30, 150

M

Mark
  10:43–45, 145
  12:28–31, 144
Matthew
  6:33, 60
  12:40–41, 136
  22:40, 144
  28:6, 142
mercy, 3, 9
Meshach, 127
Moses, 15, 19, 23, 27, 34, 82

N

Naomi, 45
Nazarites, 42
Nebuchadnezzar, 127
negative thoughts, 167–168
Nehemiah, 69
  3:5, 69
New International Version (NIV), xi, xiii
New Testament, xi, 23, 141
Ninevah, 135
Northern Kingdom, 59
Numbers, 27

O

obedience, 135–136, 173–175
Old Testament, xi, 31, 155
overlooked, feeling of being, 11–13

P

pain, 79–80, 120–121
palm trees, 92–93
Paul, 158, 161
peace, 79–80
peer pressure, 127–128
persecution, 152–153
Philippians
  4:6–7, 110
  4:7, 95
Philistines, 42
prayer, 110–111, 117, 167, 177–178
priorities, 138–139
Priscilla, 155
Promised Land, 15, 19, 34–36, 38, 42
Proverbs, 98
  1:2–3, 98
  1:7, 98
  4:7, 98
  4:7–9, 100
  16:20, 156
  25:2, 72
Proverbs 31 woman, 102–104
Psalms, 82
  19, 82
  42, 86
  42:11, 87
  66:11–12, 89
  92:7, 92
  131:2, 95
  133:2, 95
purpose, 11–13, 72–73

R

Rahab, 38, 40
refuge cities, 31
refuge in God, 31–32
rejection, 152–153
relationships
   friendships, 62–64
   with God, 3, 42–43, 95–96, 131–133
   romantic, 106–108
repentance, 52–53, 136
revelation, 82
Revelation, 177
   21, 180
   21:4, 182
righteousness, 23, 92–93
Romans
   12:9, 158
   12:9–21, 158
   12:10, 158
Ruth, 45–46

S

sacrifice, 7
Salmon, 40
salvation, 117, 136
Samson, 42
Samuel, 49
1 Samuel
   13:14, 52
2 Samuel
   11, 52
Sarah, 9
Satan, 75, 152
Saul, 52, 62
Shadrach, 127
sin, 3, 23, 59, 141, 161–162
Solomon, 52, 59, 98, 106–108, 108

Song of Solomon, 106
   1:3, 106
   1:6, 106
   2:4, 106
   2:14, 106
   2:16, 106
   3:11, 106
   8:4, 106
Southern Kingdom, 59
Spurgeon, Charles, 131–132
substitutionary atonement, 141–142
suffering, 75–77, 79–80, 120–121

T

Tarshish, 135
temptations, 161–162
2 Timothy
   1:7, 170
   4:7–8, 152
Tower of Babel, 3
trials, 89–90
trust, 3–5, 7–9, 13, 49, 66–67, 110–111

U

uniqueness, 164–165
ups and downs of life, 55–57

V

Valley of Achor (Valley of Trouble), 131

W

will of God, 177–178
wisdom, 98–100
witnessing, 117–118
woman, Proverbs 31, 102–104
Word of God, hearing, 173–175
worldly things, 148–150
worry, 66–67

ACKNOWLEDGMENTS

I would like to thank my youth pastors Scotty and Casey Gibbons, and Matt and Sarah Blankenship, who shared the Gospel with me and walked alongside me so faithfully. To this day you still impact my life, and I am forever grateful for your ministry.

I also appreciate the investment of the youth pastors and leaders of today who continue to pour into a generation that I believe is hungry for Truth. In particular, Ryan Zafiroff and Katie Anderson, who are flourishing in their callings and brought that to this book. Thank you for your prayers and your dedication to youth, which inspired me in my writing, and in seeing to the accuracy of the theology in this book.

And thank you to Theos Youth—you are doing something radically different for today's youth because you believe they matter, they care about theology, and they are capable of digesting more than most give them credit for.

ABOUT THE AUTHOR

**Brittany Rust** is a Bible teacher who is passionate about seeing people not only impacted by God's Word but also inspired to be thoughtful students of Scripture. She is the founder of Truth and Grace Ministries and the author of seven books, in addition to being an ordained minister.

Brittany lives with her family in Springfield, Missouri.

You can learn more at brittanyrust.com. You can find her on Instagram @brittanyrust, on Facebook as brittanyrustofficial, and on X @brittany_rust.